Economic Empowerment Through the Church: A Blueprint for Pro... *sive Community Development* has my endorsement and highest ... ommendation as a forward-thinking treatise as well as a road n ... on how to implement various programs to address the ma ... needs of the community through the church.

Bishop P. A. Broo ...
National General Boai ...
Church of God in Chri:

Economic Empowerment Through the Church is a wonderful and thorough tool for African-American churches in the United States. It contains invaluable information that will indeed empower those churches that find themselves in the forefront of economic development in their communities and churches wanting to help save their communities through economic redevelopment. It is a "must read" for those who are serious about [going beyond] the pulpit to do one of the most important ministries around . . . that of economic salvation and empowerment.

Lloyd Gite
Black Enterprise Magazine

I consider *Economic Empowerment Through the Church* a bible of economic empowerment that will transform the lives of Americans in the twenty-first century. It is the best how-to manual regarding economic power for the church that I have read.

The Reverend James Holley
Little Rock Baptist Church
Detroit, Michigan

Economic Empowerment Through the Church is a very much needed book. I expect it to be well received and widely used. The blunt questions, Why to do; How to do; and What to do in economic development in the church, are clearly addressed and illustrated. I want to thank Attorney Reed for the valuable addition to the resources for churches to do economic development.

John Hurst Adams
Senior Bishop—AME Church
Founder and Chairman Emeritus
Congress of National Black Churches

Economic Empowerment Through the Church is an inspiration as it provides the church with the infrastructure with which to transform human lives through step-by-step guides. When followed, these measures will lead the church to economic empowerment to rebuild the communities to which they minister. I believe that if the churches were to take advantage of only a fraction of the information contained in [this] book, they would find themselves even with, or ahead of, the "economic empowerment" game.

Ray K. Schull
Executive Vice-President
The Hannah Group

In this timely and pioneering work, Attorney Greg Reed has provided the nuts and bolts of the legal information that will enable every congregation to lay a sure foundation for its redemptive ministry to the community. Because of his work, no congregation ever need wonder again about perplexing legal questions relative to its ministry or its community service mission. Mr. Reed has extended a service of high value for all Christian churches.

The Reverend James C. Perkins
Greater Christ Baptist Church
Detroit, Michigan

E CONOMIC EMPOWERMENT THROUGH THE CHURCH

E CONOMIC EMPOWERMENT THROUGH THE CHURCH

A Blueprint for Progressive Community Development

GREGORY J. REED

FOREWORD BY C. ERIC LINCOLN

Zondervan Publishing House

Grand Rapids, Michigan

A Division of HarperCollins *Publishers*

This publication is designed to provide accurate and authoritative information in regard to the subject matter covered. It is sold with the understanding that the author and publisher are not engaged in rendering legal, accounting, or other professional service. Laws vary from state to state, and if legal advice or other expert assistance is required, the services of a competent professional should be sought.

The author and publisher specifically disclaim any liability, loss, or risk, personal or otherwise, which is incurred as a consequence, directly or indirectly, of the use and application of any of the contents of this book.

Economic Empowerment through the Church
Copyright © 1993, 1994 by Gregory J. Reed
Zondervan edition 1994

Previously published by author under the title *Progressive Clergy*

Requests for further information should be addressed to:
Zondervan Publishing House
Grand Rapids, Michigan 49530.

Cover design by Multnomah Graphics

Library of Congress Cataloging-in-Publication Data

Reed, Gregory J.
    Economic empowerment through the church : a blueprint for
progressive community development / Gregory J. Reed.
      p.   cm.
    ISBN 0-310-48951-2 (pbk.)
    1. Church finance. 2. Community development—Religious aspects—
Christianity. 3. Afro-American churches.   I. Title.
    BV770.R44   1994
    254.8—dc20   94–1895
                                                                  CIP

Printed in the United States of America

94 95 96 97 98 99 00 01 02 /❖DH/ 10 9 8 7 6 5 4 3 2 1

God…

I dedicate this book to my daughters,
Ashley S. and Arian S. Reed,
and their mother, Verladia Reed,
with thanks for their love and support.

CONTENTS

Foreword
The Progressive Mission
of the Black Church

C. Eric Lincoln
William Rand Kenan Professor of Religion, Duke University

"Wholistic" is a word mentioned frequently today whenever the ministry and mission of the black church are discussed. What it means is that the black church has begun to re-focus its attention on the critical needs of the whole individual and the whole community rather than on just spiritual or religious needs. I say "re-focus," because in the early days of the church a wholistic ministry was taken for granted; there were no alternatives for African American Christians because religious needs always included survival, or common, needs, as well as spiritual needs. There can be no religion without survival, so a wholistic ministry, to be progressive, must be addressed to both the spiritual and the physical well-being of the person or the community, or a vital interest of the mission of the church will not be accomplished.

The church's concern for the whole person is anchored quite firmly in the teachings and the ministry of Jesus Christ. The Bible tells us that "Jesus went about doing good," which means that Jesus had an active concern for the welfare of other people. That concern took as many different forms as there were different needs to be met. He fed those who were hungry; he gave sight to the blind; he strengthened the lame so that they might walk again; he comforted the sick and bereaved; and he cast out the devils of those who were mentally disturbed. All these were survival needs, but in the ministry of Jesus they were part and parcel of his spiritual mission to prepare his followers for a place with him in heaven. "He opened his mouth and taught them," but he knew then what every effective pastor knows today, that the souls to be saved are first in *this* world, and that they come clothed in flesh. The early Christian church was aware of this reality, for it was especially careful to protect its members as much as possible from the hostile Roman environment where their lives and their welfare were always in jeopardy. The early Christians lived for the faith and for each other. That was the only way they could survive, and because they did, the life-giving gospel was eventually heard in every corner of the world, and the life of the spirit became universal.

The black church too has always known the necessity and the effectiveness of a wholistic, or total, approach to its commitment to human salvation. If the Roman environment in which the early church emerged was mean and hostile, then the environment in which the early black church had to struggle was nothing short of catastrophic. It was a slave environment in which there was no freedom, no legal redress, no health protection, no social services to buffer the needs for counseling, child welfare, housing, employment, or financial assistance no matter how desperate the circumstance. Black people did not own anything, not even themselves. Even their spiritual nurture was in the hands of others who put their personal economic interests before any interests of black people, spiritual or otherwise, would be considered.

Slavery was a total way of life. There was no room in it for happenstance. And yet, because there is no need for happenstance where there is faith and enlightened determination, the black church defied the hostilities that forbade it to be born, overcame the repression that sought to destroy it, and survived to become the seed-bed and the mother of the African American culture we cherish and struggle to preserve as our heritage. The black church knows the power of a wholistic commitment by experience, for it was born of a vast schedule of needs that a nation committed to slavery could not, or would not address. Those needs were spiritual in the first instance, of course, but they were also physical, social, psychological, and economic. They were the same needs we recognize today as necessary to a reasonably dignified human existence. Since the black church was the only institution available to African Americans, it was by necessity all things to all people. The black churches gave spiritual refuge and reassurance, but they also spawned the first black banks, burial societies, insurance companies, schools, and homes for the aged as support services to the spiritual needs of their people.

As America gradually opened its doors to include African Americans in selected benefits of citizenship, the black church gradually reduced (and sometimes forgot) the survival aspects of its ministry, and became focused almost exclusively on the life to come. We know now that such a determination was premature. Our secular institutions cannot be relied upon to guard with the commitment of Christian love the humanitarian interests of all the people. Only the church can do that.

THE PROGRESSIVE MISSION OF THE BLACK CHURCH

As part of a comprehensive study of the black church, I once asked the Reverend Gardner Taylor what he perceived to be the critically unique business of the church that set it apart from all other institutions. His answer was immediate and unequivocal, suggesting that he had long since wrestled with precisely that issue and had long since resolved it with confidence and conviction. "The business of the church," he said, "is to present the souls of believers at the throne of grace with the reasonable assurance that they will be found acceptable." When I asked him his strategy for accomplishing that objective, he replied: "There is no substitute for a good role model." This brief exchange with one of the great religious leaders of our time has kept coming back to me over the years, and each time I re-live it, the clearer it becomes to me that in that handful of simple words the true mission of the church is laid out without ambiguity, and that the proper strategy for achieving that mission begins where all effective strategies begin—*with the leadership up front.* Here was a philosophy, or as Dr. Taylor would more likely have put it, a plan of work that did not strangle itself with the strictures of doctrine or the inhibitions of convention. The critical task is the "preparation and the presentation of human souls," and the methodology is by example. This allows for a spectrum of possibilities broad enough to cover all of humankind in whatever condition of being they may be found, an option of the most critical significance in any serious ministry for these times.

Such a broad-based, enlightened approach to the business of the church is particularly redemptive and progressive for the African American community that still struggles under an enormous burden of stress and instability. Change is a feature of every society, but when change is very rapid and sustained, even when considered favorable, many people lose the ability to cope. What is familiar and understood is suddenly replaced by what is unfamiliar and not understood. When change is too rapid and too pervasive, a deep (and often catastrophic) anxiety may wreak havoc with personal stability and individual responsibility.

Religion has always been civilization's most reliable answer to the trauma of change because religion is anchored in "that which changeth not," or "that which is the same yesterday, today, and forever." The church always perceives itself to be built on that rock of stability that transcends change. However, to sustain its effectiveness the church must always be alert to the need for new aspects of ministry the vagaries of change may produce. It's mission, that is to say the business of the church, remains, or ought to remain the same, but the responsible church as a unity of believers in a changing world has no mission if it does not resonate with the realities that condition the lives and circumstances of the people it exists to serve.

As these "conditioning realities" grow increasingly challenging and more demanding of multiple responses, the mission of the church is made more comprehensive. There is no need to rehearse here the litany of evils the church in general, and the black church in particular, is now called on to address, but to present a few of them even in the euphemistic code phrases we have designed to blunt their horror offers some perspective to the task we face: children having children, black males as endangered species, perpetual welfare mothers, the enormously disproportionate incarceration of black youth, homelessness, cocaine, AIDS, unemployment, and *ad infinitum*.

Some will be quick to point out that all or most of these concerns are the business of society and not properly the business of the church. But in Dr. Gardner Taylor's lexicon of mission, the business of the church cannot always be separated from the business of society for a man or a woman is both soul *and* body, and to salvage the one often requires healing the other. This is good practical theology properly informed with the social consciousness of the Sermon on the Mount. But it is a theology that requires empowerment, both spiritual and economic. Unfortunately, the strategies of economic empowerment are not included in the seminary curriculums on which we rely for the training of church leadership. That problem is exacerbated for black clergy who characteristically need it most because they seldom have access to family traditions of economic empowerment to call upon in situations of crisis.

Economic empowerment is a reasonable response to the fact that we are presently in the world, if not of it, and being in the world requires the full armor of the faith to survive. The auxiliaries of the spiritual quest: schools, retirement homes, drug clinics, employment services, well-baby clinics, credit unions, affordable housing and the like are also the "business" of the church because the business of the church remains what it always was, ministering to the whole person and the whole community.

The black church takes in well over two billion dollars a year in dues, donations, and charitable giving. It also receives many times that figure in voluntary services and other "in kind" contributions. At least seventy-five percent of all African American charitable giving goes to the black church, and yet the black church as an institution is always on the edge of insolvency. Forty-five percent of all African American ministers must work at part- or full-time jobs outside the church in order to sustain themselves and their families, and the average urban church carries a mortgage of $63,000. Some churches have mortgage encumbrances of hundreds of thousands of dollars, of course, which tends to suggest an injudicious imbalance between the building or buying of real estate and the real needs of the congregation and its ability to pay. But there are other hazards of which poor record-keeping, haphazard fiscal policy, and a generalized impatience with the legal and business aspects of the necessary interface with the world outside the church are the most frequent.

In pursuit of the spiritual realm, the pastor who forgets, or who ignores the fact that his basic responsibilities must begin where the people are, does so at his peril, and at the peril of his parish. The black church is poor, but it is still a multi-billion dollar enterprise, and its poverty does not have to be a characteristic feature of its existence. An effective ministry today requires effective funding *and* effective stewardship. Since the black church is by all odds the best-funded institution in the black community, and since the spectrum of African American needs continues to broaden and to escalate, effective stewardship in the black church can no longer ignore the call to black economic empowerment and still claim responsible leadership. We are poised for freedom, or we are programmed for disaster. The time for new directions is now. In other crises such as education and civil rights, when all else failed, the people turned to the black church and the church made heroic history for itself and for its people. Now the black churches face the gravest challenge of all: The challenge to sustain with economic empowerment the hard-won freedoms that came with open access to education and the legal availability of civil rights. It is quite clear that none of the freedoms we cherish can survive in a vacuum of economic deprivation, and that spiritual redemption begins with a full stomach, a warm place to sleep, and a hope for something better than perpetual handouts.

As the mission of the black church continues to broaden its perspectives to cover the whole spectrum of humanitarian needs within and beyond its membership, it will of course require increasingly sophisticated leadership skills at the top. It will find them in the bright young men and women now in the seminaries, and in the increasing number of second-career men and women who are entering Christian service after successful careers in business or the professions. The social crises we now face in the community should produce no crisis of leadership in the move toward economic empowerment. The strong, ingenious traditional black ministers who have brought the black church thus far by faith have worked miracles. When almost all the mainline white denominations are in decline from the ravages of a civilization lurched out of control, the black church has held its own, and with occasional distinction. The progressive church today needs but recognize and utilize the accumulating resources at hand and waiting for assignment to move forward in its mission for earth and heaven alike. A lawyer, a teacher, an accountant, a securities broker, or a banker need not be ordained to share the burden of leadership in the church. They only need to be invited. Paul's doctrine of using whatever talent the membership possesses is a good one for these times.

This is a handbook for the economic empowerment the black church needs to equip itself for service beyond the spiritual and protect itself and its membership in the process. We are generally agreed that economic empowerment and community development are necessary for black survival, but few church leaders know how to go about either. Our gospel choirs are the best there are, but how do we get them on records and tapes and discs? The great sermons, the moral uplift, the community outreach that emanates from our pulpits deserve the widest possible audience, but what are the techniques, the pros and cons, and the cost of radio or television broadcasting? How, when, and by what means should church personnel be compensated? And what are the false steps a church can make that may cause it to lose its tax exemption? When may individuals be sued for things they did or did not do as church members? And when may an excessive salary paid to the minister place the whole church in legal jeopardy? How may the churches purchase insurance, supplies, goods and services collectively, conserving millions of dollars needed for black economic improvement? The answer to questions like these are not taught in seminaries, yet these are the answers the progressive black church needs for a relevant ministry in the world we know today.

The most progressive church leadership all across the country is rethinking its priorities and networking to the commitment of serving the whole person. In Atlanta, the Wheat Street Baptist Church sponsors a federal credit union which has over a period of four decades provided one-and-a-half million dollars in loans for African Americans without access to other financial institutions. In Oakland, California, co-pastors J. Alfred Smith and J. Alfred Smith, Jr. led the Allen Temple Baptist church in sponsoring a seventy-five unit housing development for the elderly, fifty-one additional unrestricted units, a credit union with one million dollars in assets, a blood bank, and other projects vital to community service. Allen AME Church in Jamaica, New York, pastored by Congressman Floyd Flake, Jr., is deeply involved in multi-family housing, an oil consortium, a credit union, and an accredited school for students from kindergarten to tenth grade. Abyssinian Baptist Church in

Harlem owns the Abyssinian Development Corporation, which operates hundreds of units of housing in Harlem and has been a vital force in community revitalization. Other institutional churches such as Antioch Missionary Baptist Church in Chicago, Union Baptist Church in Baltimore, Metropolitan Baptist in Memphis, Hartford Avenue Baptist in Detroit, and Concord Baptist Church in Brooklyn have become landmark institutions in the wholistic religious service that includes economic empowerment and black economic development. Some churches have pooled their assets in the interest of a more comprehensive service than any one church could accomplish alone. In North Philadelphia, the Hope Plaza Shipping Center, built by the Deliverance Evangelistic Church, includes a Thriftway Supermarket, a two-story McDonalds, and other stores. The Linwood Shopping Center in Kansas City, Missouri was born of the joint efforts of more than 100 ministers from dozens of churches in the Kansas City area. After only six years experience in economic development, the Linwood Alliance has initiated a second retail complex for small minority businesses.

What these churches have done, other churches can do. The time for looking to others to do for us what we can do for ourselves is past. It will not return. The strategies for economic empowerment are not included in the seminary courses but are included in this text which shall be considered, over the course of time, to be the "bible" of economic empowerment for the church: a blueprint for progressive community development.

This volume should go a long way in asking the questions and supplying the answers necessary to carry a proud tradition of effective black church Christian service on into the twenty-first century of its existence. The black church is the soul of America, and if America is to save its soul, it is time to be up and about it.

Acknowledgments

The author wishes to express his sincere appreciation for Elan Sandelin's timely research, which was critical to certain parts of this book as well as the cover design by Brenda D. Stroud.

Special recognition is also due Mr. Don Davis, Chairman of First Independence National Bank, who helped to spark the completion of this book. Thanks to Anthony Adams and Michael Josey for their contributions and input on community and economic development and wrongful discharge, respectively, and how it affects churches today. Also, thanks to Carl R. Edwards, Esq., for his support and helpful comments.

Special thanks to my mother Bertha, Maureen Pearson, Alma Whittley, Maurita Coley, Esq., Mark Macon, Dr. Leroy Johnson, Dr. Oswald Bostic, Jean Mair, Larkin Arnold, Esq., Reuben Cannon, Rachel Woods, Sharon Lawson, Norwaine Reed, Stephanie Hammonds, Esq., Williams Gibbons, Jack Martin, Allan Young, Christina Arnold, Richard Manson, Esq., Dr. C. Eric Lincoln ... **Malcolm X and Dr. Betty Shabazz ... Rosa Parks . . . Martin Luther King, Jr. . . .**

I would also like to acknowledge the following individuals for their efforts and inspiration both directly and indirectly: Rev. Edgar Vann, Rev. Revely (Messiah MBC), Dr. T. B. Boyd III, Rev. Nyathi (Hartford Memorial Baptist Church), Bishop Brooks (St. Paul), Rev. James Perkins (Greater Christ Baptist Church), Rev. Jim Holley (Little Rock MBC), Rev. W. Smith (Rose of Sharon), Rev. Jim Wadsworth (Fellowship Chapel), Rev. Sampson (Tabernacle), Rev. J. L. Webb (New Mt. Vernon Baptist Church), Rev. Jack Boland (Church of Today), Hon. Jackie Vaughn III, Hon. Teola P. Hunter, Hon. Adam Shakoor, William Gibbons, Benet McMillan, Esq., Linda Jones, Lee Ivory, Joyce C. Thomas, Willie Wofford, Edward Hubbard, Esq., and Bonnie Berry, Esq.

Notable thanks to Zondervan's staff—Sam Hooks, Stan Gundry, and Ed van der Maas—for their help in bringing forth this book as a tool to transform the lives of Americans. Last but not least, a special thanks to Grace Adams. My thanks and appreciation to you all for your support in this endeavor.

Introduction

Churches have stabilized many sectors of the community over the years and have played a vital role in developing and leading the way with various institutionalized projects such as educational, self-help and self-awareness programs, and credit unions.

There is no comprehensive source or reference material available to churches explaining how to develop projects or programs. Many of them learned to develop projects through trial and error. Very few churches can point to a reference or source that can be passed on as a legacy that will enable pastors, members, and the community to use as a blueprint or a check and balance so that their present and future resources are effectively used to further develop, or enhance, existing projects.

The materials herein are designed with this purpose in mind—to perpetuate and uplift the community, to aid churches in taking the lead by stabilizing communities in both urban and rural settings. They are designed for any religious denomination and the information is applicable to all, but most particularly to the African American communities that may have strayed away from the true self-help tradition which the black church helped to create. Due to the progressive state of this country, many pastors and churches have fallen behind the times and do not have much knowledge about financial investments and economic development. In the black community, some developments have been undertaken by large elite black churches that are likely to have more well-educated members, activists, and astute pastors.

This book addresses some positive approaches of operation when churches do not have members with the foresight necessary to help develop and protect the church, especially the black church, in stabilizing its community. Over the years, the Roman Catholics have developed the most comprehensive educational and economic development programs. Other denominations need to learn how to do the same. Black churches, along with quasi-religious, mutual societies and fraternal orders, created significant economic institutions such as banks, insurance companies, building and loan associations, and funeral parlors during the latter nineteenth and twentieth centuries. Many churches have lost their focus. Black churches started placing more emphasis and resources in education, civil rights, integrationist issues, and developing moral character than in the economic development of people so that they can reap their just rewards on earth.

Churches are significant economic institutions. In fact, black churches raised plate offerings in excess of $1.7 billion during just one year. But the problem lies in the fact that a portion of these offerings have not been directed by the clergy to help the people that can be leveraged with greater returns in terms of jobs, housing, community improvements and the like. If this book is even *partially* used, many churches will be able to correct and develop ways to support their members and communities.

Another concern that this book seeks to address (which is a major weakness of the black church) is in the area of economics and finances. Black denominations need to address poor financial foundations and record keeping. This has been one of the key problems and sources of conflict in church disputes. The lack of proper records makes it nearly impossible for churches to plan, develop, grow, and contribute to the community.

This book will enlighten and present various methods of operation and paths which the church may utilize as a main participant in the twenty-first century.

To truly be progressive, one needs a blueprint. Therefore, this book is designed to help light the path so that the church may see and refocus its efforts, rescuing those who need support in order to help make this a healthy and progressive society.

1

Questions/Answers

To save America's soul, the ministry consciousness must be transformed to become the Progressive Clergy . . .

What follows is a list of the most commonly asked questions by those involved in the church relating to clergy and tax issues. We have written these questions and given the applicable general answers. Detailed answers to these questions can be found within the applicable sections of the book. These short answers are a guide to the general church-related tax questions that may be asked—but there is no substitute for professional assistance.

I. Church and Nonprofit Organization Start-up

Q: *What defines a church for tax purposes?*

A: The IRS does not have a specific definition of what is a church. Instead, it determines on a case-by-case basis whether a particular organization is a church.

Q: *Why should a church incorporate?*

A: Incorporation would help church members or volunteers avoid individual personal liability from any lawsuits or legal problems related to the church.

Q: *What documents are needed to begin an ecclesiastical nonprofit corporation?*

A: Articles of Incorporation, Bylaws, and Corporate Minutes.

Q: *Why should your organization have a federal Employer Identification Number (EIN)?*

A: Having an EIN will help the pastor or members of the church avoid personal liability for taxes and it distinguishes the church entity from any individual member.

II. Contributions and Donations

Q: *When are charitable contributions/donations deductible for tax purposes?*

A: Contributions are deductible when made to a church organization that has been declared tax exempt by the IRS. Items donated cannot be used or sold in a manner contrary to the church's tax-exempt status.

Q: *What organizations qualify as tax-deductible donees?*

A: Organizations that have filed the appropriate tax-exempt application and have been approved by the IRS. These organizations cannot participate in political campaigns or discriminate against any individual.

Q: *What contributions are not deductible?*

A: Gifts made that are contingent upon some act or event which may occur, and the value of volunteer labor are not deductible.

Q: *What is the IRS's position on churches in the home?*

A: Churches in the home are allowable but problems may arise in determining housing and parsonage allowances.

Q: *What forms of non-cash contributions qualify as tax-deductible contributions?*

A: Clothing, land, stocks, and other tangible or intangible items qualify. Problems arise if the contribution is income producing. Donors, also, may not be able to deduct the full value of some donations (e.g., stock). You should consult a tax attorney to determine how much is deductible.

Q: *How must contributions/donations to qualified organizations be given in order to be deemed tax-deductible?*

A: The church should allow the donor to determine the value of the item. For (non-cash) property valued over $5,000, the church must complete Part I, Section B of the donor's Internal Revenue Service Form 8283 appraisal summary. In order to claim a deduction, the tax payer must submit verified receipts for the deduction to be allowed.

Q: *What support should your organization maintain for contributions/donations received?*

A: Volunteers or paid staff should be available to receive the items, disperse receipts, and maintain records of donor-determined value of the items.

III. 501 (c)(3) Tax-Exempt Status: Why Is It So Important?

Q: *What are some of the benefits of IRS 501(c)(3) federal tax exemption?*

A: A nonprofit church that qualifies for tax-exempt status is not liable for taxes to the federal government on income (if related to their tax-exempt purpose). Donations and contributions would be tax deductible to the person donating.

Q: *Is a church required to obtain federal tax-exempt status to operate?*

A: Some states require that a church obtain tax-exempt status to operate within their boundaries. It must be noted that a church is considered to be tax-exempt irrespective of filing a tax-exempt application 1023 with the federal government. States do not and cannot grant tax-exempt status.

Q: *How does one apply for federal tax exemption?*

A: First, obtain legal counsel. Second, with the aid of legal counsel, complete the following: Articles of Incorporation, Bylaws, Minutes, and Internal Revenue Service 1023 Application. Last, mail these forms to the appropriate agencies.

Q: *What is the cost and how much time is needed to prepare the tax-exempt application?*

A: The cost is moderate. A church saves time by completing the forms with an attorney. Filing without professional help will cause problems and delays in the application process.

Q: *What is a Group Exemption?*

A: Some organizations or churches can be tax-exempt by virtue of being affiliated with a church or being a member of an association of churches.

Q: *What are the public disclosure requirements for tax-exempt organizations?*

A: All tax-exempt applications mailed after July 15, 1987, must be made available for public inspection along with IRS Form 1023 or 1024 and any letters or documents issued by the IRS in response to the tax-exempt application. Copies of the IRS

990 annual returns must also be available for public inspection during normal business hours. Penalties will be imposed for failure to comply.

Q: *What are the filing requirements for tax-exempt organizations?*

A: Tax-exempt organizations must file Form 990, an annual information report, and annual report.

Q: *May I prepare my own exempt application?*

A: Yes, you may, but it is not advisable. Most problems arise from improperly completed applications. Technical help from a tax lawyer can avert problems in the application process.

Q: *What is Unrelated Business Taxable Income?*

A: Unrelated Business Taxable Income, commonly referred to as UBI, is income earned by the church which is not related to its tax-exempt function, such as income from a bookstore, restaurant, etc.

Q: *When is UBI taxable to an exempt organization?*

A: This income is taxable if it is produced income from a trade or business, the trade or business is operated on a regular basis, and the trade or business does not relate to the church's tax-exempt function.

IV. Church/Nonprofit Accounting and IRS Compliance

Q: *What accounting procedure will ensure compliance with IRS record-keeping requirements?*

A: The church should retain any tax forms or tax returns filed for at least four years. Receipts from money spent related and not related to the tax-exempt function of the church should be retained. All records of compensation paid to non-ministerial and ministerial employees should be retained, as well as records of any rents or parsonage paid to them.

Q: *What accounts should your organization maintain in its accounting system?*

A: Payroll, Expenses, Equity (net worth), Petty Cash Fund and all Banking Accounts.

Q: *What forms and documents should be used to record financial transactions/activities?*

A: Cancelled checks, paid bills, duplicate deposit slips, balance sheets, inventory lists, and monthly/weekly summaries of income.

V. What Are the Reporting Requirements to the IRS for Churches and Other Nonprofit Organizations?

Q: *What are the reporting requirements to the IRS for churches related to unordained and ordained employees?*

A: For ordained ministers, the church must report social security tax and possibly self-employment and income tax. For unordained employees, the church must report social security, self-employment, and income taxes.

Q: *What are the church's employer record-keeping requirements?*

A: The church must keep records of employment taxes (income, social security, self-employment, and state taxes) for at least four years after the appropriate tax returns are filed. The church should record its Employer Identification Number and maintain copies of filed returns and records of deposits.

Q: *What informational returns are required?*

A: The church is required to file a tax return with the IRS accounting for how it spent its funds annually. This return should reflect any compensation paid to unordained and ordained employees. In order to maintain its tax-exempt status, it must also file an annual information report with the IRS.

Q: *How do you prepare the required information returns?*

A: These returns should be completed with the aid of tax counsel or an accountant. Most tax returns must be mailed to the IRS by April 15 of every year, but other tax forms have different filing deadlines.

VI. What Minutes Are Helpful in Substantiating Business Operations for Tax Purposes?

1. Minutes of Directors Meetings
2. Housing Allowance
3. Qualified Corporate Reimbursement Plan
4. Expense Reports
5. Directors' Meeting Notices
6. Liability Release Forms
7. Ministry of Helps Information Sheets, etc.
8. Employment Agreement for the Minister

VII. IRS and Church Audits

Q: *Does the IRS have the right to audit the church?*

A: Yes, if it has reasonable belief that improper activities are being conducted by the church.

Q: *Under what circumstances are church inquiries and examinations made under IRS Code Section 7611?*

A: An inquiry can begin only when a U.S. Department of Treasury official reasonably believes, based on facts and circumstances, recorded in writing that
   1. The church may be engaged in activities subject to tax,
   2. The church may not qualify for tax exemption as a church,
   3. The church failed to answer routine IRS inquiries or questions, or
   4. The church is conducting trade or business unrelated to its tax-exempt function.

Q: *What procedures must the IRS perform in order to audit your church?*

A: The IRS must give the church Notice of Church Tax Inquiry; 15 days after this notice is mailed, the IRS must give Notice of Examination. The Notice of Examination must be mailed at least 15 days before the date of the examination. The IRS has two years to make a decision on the issue in question, but this period can be extended.

Q: *What records can the IRS examine?*

A: The IRS can examine all records on the church premises and any church-related records held by third parties.

Q: *What is the purpose of an IRS audit?*

A: The purpose of an IRS audit is to determine whether a church qualifies for tax-exempt status, or whether the church is involved in unrelated business, or is otherwise subject to be taxed or liable for additional taxes. If a church loses its exempt status, it may owe the IRS back taxes, with interest and penalties.

Q: *What role does private inurement play in IRS audits?*

A: A nonprofit organization is not supposed to operate for the benefit of an individual. If the IRS determines that an individual is deriving inurement from the tax-exempt organization, then the organization will lose its exempt status.

Q: *What are some additional tax facts and issues that should be highlighted?*

A: Churches should make sure that they do not overcompensate employees or ministers. Excessive compensation is regarded as an individual inurement.

VIII.   Minister's Personal Tax Return

Q: *Are you a qualified minister of the gospel for tax purposes?*

A: If you are "duly ordained, commissioned, or a licensed minister of a church," and you are a practicing staff member who performs religious services or functions that are considered ministerial duties in your particular church, then you qualify as a minister for tax purposes.

Q: *How do you establish the housing parsonage allowances?*

A: The church should create a budget to allocate the proper amount of housing allowance needed. The allowance should not be excessive.

Q: *How do you handle housing and parsonage allowances properly?*

A: Any parsonage amount paid to the minister should be duly recorded and reported on the church's records and the minister's individual tax return.

Q: *Who qualifies for such an allowance?*

A: An ordained minister qualifies if he does not already own the housing provided. Non-ordained employees qualify for a housing allowance if housing is provided on the church's business premises, if it is provided for the convenience of the church, and/or if it is a condition of the person's employment.

Q: *How do you account for housing and parsonage allowance expenses?*

A: All housing allowances paid out should be recorded and reported in the church's books and records.

Q: *What is the employment status of your minister: employee or self-employed?*

A: The determination of whether a minister is employed or self-employed is ultimately made by the IRS, not the church. The church can submit a Form SS-8 to the IRS, and it will determine if an individual is an employee or self-employed. The IRS criteria depends upon the amount of control that the church has over the minister's performance of his duties. If the church controls how, when, and where a minister performs his duties, then he will generally be regarded as an employee.

Q: *Should a minister who has been designated an employee pay the self-employment tax?*

A: If a minister is designated an employee by the IRS, he should *not* pay self-employment taxes. The minister may elect to be exempt from paying self-employment taxes by filing Form 4361 with the Internal Revenue Service. A minister should enlist the aid of a tax attorney when determining whether he should or should not pay self-employment taxes.

2

Organizing the Church Structure

Let us do first things first.
The Lord always provides; be patient.

A church has the option to be an unincorporated association or to become a corporation. An unincorporated association is an informal gathering of people with like interests and purpose(s). In contrast, a corporation is an "artificial person or legal entity" that is recognized by law. Each of these two organizational formats have their advantages and disadvantages. The distinctions between the two involve differences in personal liability, legal status, and organizational requirements.

Most churches begin as unincorporated associations with a few members and move on to the incorporated stage. This is due to fears resulting from a lack of understanding and information surrounding the incorporation process. From a legal perspective, a corporation is the best entity under which a church should conduct its affairs. It should be noted that both unincorporated associations and corporations can be tax-exempt if proper procedures are followed.

Unincorporated Associations

Unincorporated associations make up the vast majority of churches across the country. The question of whether to become incorporated can be decided by the church or can be dictated by state laws. Some states do not allow churches to become incorporated, while other states require a church to do so.[1] The laws regarding whether a church can be incorporated vary from state to state. The church's representative should consult its legal advisor or contact its state licensing department for the state's requirements.

Though unincorporated associations are similar to partnerships, they are not identical. Unincorporated associations usually have more members and different focuses than partnerships. States occasionally treat an unincorporated association as a corporation, especially for legal matters.

Beware of the Association Format

Many churches may find the unincorporated association status undesirable because of the liability to which its members are exposed. In an unincorporated association, each member can be viewed as an owner or having an interest in the association. As an owner or interest holder, each member of the board of trustees, officers, or individual members can be sued individually if a legal problem arises involving the association. This possibly includes liability that may arise from non-filing of tax returns or the negligent performance of duties by the association's agents or employees who may have been acting within the scope of their employment. If the association can be sued by law, its members can be sued as well.

Being unincorporated leaves an association's members vulnerable to lawsuits, legal and tax problems of the church which they probably did not anticipate when they joined the association. Once one is aware, the potential for personal liability can discourage membership in an association. It is uncertain as to how far an association may go to protect the personal rights of its members by legal action.[2] Churches should consider the legal consequences when deciding whether to remain unincorporated or become a corporation.

Corporations

Compared to the unincorporated format, a corporate structure is the most feasible entity under which to conduct business. The individuals who are members of an incorporated church organization are substantially less vulnerable to personal liability or lawsuits. The corporation, for liability purposes, is considered separate and distinct from the individuals who comprise it. Therefore, if an incorporated church is sued, its members will not be legally involved.

Individuals or church members are better protected in a corporation than they are in an unincorporated entity. For this reason, a church should seriously consider becoming an incorporated entity. The protection described may enable a corporation to successfully solicit membership and provide its members with a general sense of security in volunteering their services. Consequently, a major lawsuit against an unincorporated association could liquidate the assets of the association, as well as the assets of its members.

A corporation also differs in other aspects from an unincorporated organization. A church may simply exist normally to be considered an unincorporated association, but in order for a church to become a corporation, certain legal steps must be taken. Governmental approval must be granted. Therefore, a church desiring to become incorporated must file a certificate of incorporation with the Secretary of State or licensing bureau of its state. A payment of a nominal filing fee is required to initiate the process. The incorporation certificate should be completed with the aid of an attorney to avoid errors. Failure to properly complete all necessary forms may result in denial of corporate status.

Incorporation Requirements

The contents of a certificate of incorporation vary from state to state, but there are some general requirements which must be observed, such as

1. The organization must file as a domestic not-for-profit/nonprofit entity,
2. The proposed name of the corporation must be provided. Naming the entity is subject to some restrictions (e.g., deceptive names or names already incorporated cannot be used),
3. A statement of the purpose of the organization must be provided,
4. A statement of the nonprofit nature of the organization must be included,
5. A statement barring "prohibited" (self-serving) transactions shall be included (this is necessary to obtain tax-exempt status),
6. The location of the corporate office must be included,
7. The number of directors or trustees is required in certain states (some states stipulate the minimum and the maximum numbers),
8. The name and address of the designated resident agent for service of process must be provided. (This is the person who can receive

notice of a lawsuit against the organization.) The majority of states require that such a person be designated, and

9. The signature(s) of approval from the required incorporation official must be provided.[3]

Minutes and resolutions must also be maintained by the church for setting goals and maintaining orderly or official acts of the church. The church and its attorney should contact the Secretary of State or the licensing bureau to inquire about the particular requirements for its state. If a request for incorporation is denied, a church can appeal to its state court system.[4]

Unincorporated Association and Corporate Requirements

An *unincorporated* association or organization has similar rules which govern it. Both require a set of guidelines by which the membership and governing body should adhere to as directed by the board of directors or trustees that manages the association. The internal management of the association should be determined by the association and reflected in the following documents:

1. Articles of association (should be tailored to fit the association's purposes and plans), which must include the following:
   a. The name of the association
   b. A statement of its purpose
   c. The powers of its managing body and its duties (including directors, trustees, officers, and committees)
   d. Proper expulsion and resignation procedures
   e. The process to amend the constitution or bylaws[5]
2. A constitution
3. A set of bylaws[6]

An *incorporated* organization should have comparable guidelines. The articles for a corporation, however, should be drafted with the aid of an attorney to avoid legal problems in the future. The bylaws of an association or a corporation should include these items:

1. A statement of the purpose of the organization (in great detail)
2. A statement of qualifications for membership
3. A statement describing the duties, powers, qualifications, and compensation of all officers, trustees, directors, etc.
4. A statement stipulating all fiscal matters

5. The procedures for amendments to the constitution and the bylaws.[7]

Some states stipulate exactly what the bylaws of a corporation or association must include. A church may inquire of the regulatory agency in its state as to what these stipulations may be.

Conclusion

A church must consider many things when deciding whether to be an unincorporated association versus an incorporated entity. The basic organizational guidelines of each are similar. They both should have a charter (or articles) or a constitution and bylaws. The two types of organizations, however, differ greatly on the issue of personal liability of their members. An unincorporated association is identified by its members; consequently, these members are very vulnerable to personal liability or lawsuits. In contrast, a corporation is recognized as a fictitious individual, so its members are not automatically subject to individual liability. No matter which avenue a church decides to take, it must be aware that the only way to legally be considered a nonprofit organization one hundred percent (100%) is to obtain tax-exempt status by submitting a 1023 application to the IRS.

To receive this status, the church must follow various federal and state governmental guidelines and complete specific forms. Failure to follow the particular rules of the federal government and the state (domicile of the church) can cause a church not to secure or to lose tax-exempt status. Governmentally imposed fines could result. To protect itself, the church should always have a representative seek legal advice when deciding whether to remain an unincorporated association or become incorporated.

3

Tax Planning

We have all the things that enable us to do what we need to do.
We just need to know how to use them.

There are a large number of churches in the United States today, most of which have benefited from the privilege of tax exemption provided by the federal government. There is a complex set of rules that govern the area of tax exemption which can impact the church's business operation:

1. Affecting whether a church is audited
2. Deciding what is unrelated business income
3. Showing how to properly prepare and file minister compensation
4. Addressing social security taxation
5. Fighting discrimination

These functions relate to a church's tax-exempt status. Any problems with tax-exempt status can lead to a church losing its exempt status and owing the federal government back taxes with penalties and interest. There are certain tax issues a church must be aware of to avoid being audited or having its tax-exempt status revoked.

AVOIDING TAX PROBLEMS

How does an Internal Revenue Service inquiry get started? Churches should be aware that under the 1984 Tax Reform Act, the IRS was given the authority to conduct church audits.8 There are two principle instances that may initiate a church audit. The first is when an appropriate high-level treasury official receives information in writing that may reasonably suggest that a church

1. Is carrying on trade or business activities that are not related to its tax-exempt function,
2. Is engaged in activities subject to tax, or
3. Does not qualify for tax-exemption as a church.

When a treasury official receives such information in writing, an inquiry can be made. The information that is "received in writing" can come from any source. It can come from a published article in the media or via a complaint from a former employee or a disgruntled member.

Another instance in which a church audit may be induced is when a church fails to comply with certain tax law requirements or fails to furnish certain information requested by the IRS. Such failure to comply may include

1. Failure to file a tax return,
2. Failure to comply with income tax, FICA (Social Security), tax withholding or filing requirements,
3. Failure to properly supply information needed to justify an incorrectly filed return,
4. Failure to provide information that is used to compile the Internal Revenue publication, the *Cumulative List of Organizations*[9] (which provides a list of all qualified charitable organizations in the United States), or
5. Failure to confirm that a specific business is or is not owned or operated by the church.

A church cannot question the reasonableness of the IRS inquiry. Once the inquiry has begun, the church can only dispute the IRS inquiries if proper procedures are not being followed. If a church fails to comply with two or more of these routine questions or inquiries, the IRS will have sufficient basis to begin an official examination. Therefore, if the Internal Revenue Service decides to examine a church entity, there is no recourse. Once an examination begins there are particular rules governing how the audit must be conducted. The Notice of Examination cannot be mailed until 15 days after the date of the Notice of Church Tax Inquiry is mailed, and it must be mailed at least 15 days before the date of examination.[10]

The Notice of Examination must contain

1. A copy of the church tax inquiry notice,
2. A description of the church records and activities the IRS seeks to examine,
3. An offer of a conference between the church and the IRS to resolve concerns relating to the examination,
4. A copy of all documents collected or prepared by the IRS for use in the examination, and
5. The Notice must be signed by the Commissioner.[11]

The Internal Revenue Service has two years during which it must make a decision concerning the issue in question.[12] Unfortunately for churches, this two-year period is not limited to calendar years. If the church engages in litigation against the IRS, the two-year period is suspended. Also, if the IRS exceeds the two-year limit, "the only penalty is a stay of proceedings in a summons proceeding in order to gain access to church records until the requirements are satisfied."[13] This means that the examination does not terminate at the close of two years; the close of this period merely makes it more difficult for the IRS to gain access to church records.

During an examination, all the records of a church are open for review by the IRS agent. Temporary regulations also allow the IRS to examine all third-party records such as bank statements, and are free of any restrictions. Furthermore, "the IRS is not only required to examine records that pertain to its inquiry,"[14] but also any and all records may be examined to determine if the church can maintain its exempt status.[15] Therefore, churches should keep in mind that the Internal Revenue Service can begin a church audit for a variety of reasons. Once the audit has begun, there is little that the church can do to stop it. Therefore, it is very important for a church to conduct its financial activities in a way that is above reproach and follow the proper tax laws.

Unrelated Business Income

All tax-exempt organizations need funds to conduct operations. Funds are usually obtained through nontaxable charitable contributions or income-producing activities. It is the income-producing activities that typically cause the most tax problems for churches. Income-producing activities of a tax-exempt organization are subject to taxation at the federal corporate rate if the activities satisfy certain criteria.

The three key criteria that trigger taxation are these:

1. The income is produced from a trade or business,

2. The income activity, trade, or business is continued on a regular basis, and
3. The operation of such trade or business is not substantially related to the church's tax-exempt purpose.[16]

Income which meets these three criteria is known as Unrelated Business Income (UBI). Unrelated Business Income is usually taxable even to tax-exempt organizations, including churches. Production of this type of income can jeopardize a church's tax-exempt status. Therefore, churches should be extremely careful to avoid producing UBI. The UBI general rule does have several exceptions which a church can take advantage of without jeopardizing its tax-exempt status.

Trade or Business

The first key criterion forces churches to consider, "What is a trade or business?" A trade or business is "any activity carried on for the production of income from the sale of goods or the performance of services."[17] Examples of trades and businesses carried on by a nonprofit entity such as a church which can be subject to tax are

1. Laundromats
2. Fast-food operations
3. Senior citizens' housing
4. Bookstores
5. Clothing stores
6. Rental incomes
7. Real estate development
8. Managerial services

Sometimes an activity that does not appear to be a trade or business is exactly that. In one instance, a nonprofit organization was found to be conducting a business when it sold Christmas cards. The sale was regularly carried on with the intent to produce income. In this situation, literature was sent to individuals for the purpose of soliciting donations. Christmas cards were included in this literature package, free of obligation. Yet literature was provided for anyone who was willing to make a future offer of these same cards with a donation. This mailing was considered a trade or business which took place on a continual or regular basis. This operation was also found to be unrelated to the exempt function of the organization.

When an organization conducts an operation that goes beyond the scope of its exempt purpose for the express intent of producing income, it may be considered a trade or business subject to taxation.

Trade or Business on a Regular Basis

The second key factor for UBI is whether the activity is conducted on a regular basis with "frequency and continuity."[18] At first, this terminology may seem vague, but the regulation suggests that a comparison must be made with similar activities carried on by a profit-seeking enterprise. For instance, a church organization that randomly conducts a one-day car wash to raise funds for a particular project would not be considered a regularly conducted business. On the other hand, if the church were to operate the car wash on a consistent basis similar to that of a profit-seeking entity, it would be considered a regularly conducted trade or business.

Subsequently, what matters is the frequency and continuity with which the activities are conducted and the manner in which the activity is pursued when determining whether the activity is performed on a regular basis. For example, an annual fundraising event in the form of a series of vaudeville shows spanning one week may not be considered a regularly conducted business. The basic purpose of this test is to eliminate any unfair competition that might arise between a taxable profit-seeking entity and a nonprofit organization.

In one such case, program guides were sold at these shows, and the guides contained advertising that was not related to the association's activities.[19] Furthermore, the shows were promoted by an independent organization that was under a contract for services rendered. The court found, however, that the shows were considered "intermittent activities" that were not conducted on a regular basis and, therefore, did not produce unrelated business income. The fact that they occurred every year for one week did not constitute a continuing business. This example demonstrates that an unrelated business can be carried on if it is not a substantially regular operation within a given time period.

The criteria for determining the regularity of time that is required to constitute unrelated business income coincides with the activities of a profit-seeking entity.[20] If an organization conducts an activity without regularity, as a for-profit business might, it probably will not be considered for taxation. Therefore, many fundraising activities that a church conducts are not subject to tax. These activities include, but are not limited to,

1. Car washes
2. Bake sales
3. Bazaars
4. Carnivals
5. Fairs
6. Craft shows and the like

If a church is conducting an activity on a regular basis that is not related to its exempt function, it may have to pay taxes on such income. These activities might include, depending on the circumstances,

1. Regular rental of parking space,
2. Regular rental of the church building,
3. Regular advertising space in church bulletins or publications,
4. Regularly conducting a concession stand for a period constituting a business season or more, or
5. Regularly selling retail or manufactured merchandise with the intent to derive a profit.

Trade or Business Substantially Related to the Exempt Purpose

If income is determined to have UBI, certain deductions that would be considered ordinary and necessary in the conduct of such a business will be affected. If expenses or depreciation of an activity are attributable to both tax-exempt use and the unrelated business, special deduction allocations must be made.[21] For example, if a church gym is used by its members 50% of the time and rented to a basketball league for the remainder of the time on a regular basis, deductions related to this activity would be allocated as 50% to the unrelated business and 50% to the tax-exempt use. However, the rental to a basketball league does not necessarily constitute an unrelated business. If the league is maintained as a part of the organization's tax-exempt function, then the rental may not be UBI. To constitute UBI, the league would have to be unrelated to the exempt purpose of the church.

The activity must be related to the organization's exempt purpose in order to be considered tax-exempt. A nonrelated activity can qualify for tax-exemption only if it is incidental to the organization. In one IRS case involving the Universal Church of Jesus Christ and its director Dona Sly, the court found that the church's commercial activities were far more than incidental to its exempt activities. The activities were found to be pervasive and substantially unrelated to the organization's tax-exempt purpose.[22] The religious organization was operating a debt-collection agency, a magazine subscription clearinghouse, and a health insurance plan. In this case, not only was all the income declared taxable, but the church's exempt status was revoked.

It should be noted that the IRS can revoke an organization's exempt status on a retroactive basis.[23] This can result in an accrued liability that can include excessive penalties, interest, and back taxes.

Religious Entities
Conducting Income-Producing Activities

From the information presented above thus far, it would seem that most income-producing activities might be taxable. Such income activities might include:

1. Conducting fund-raising bazaars,
2. Conducting car washes,
3. Hosting dinners,
4. Operating clothing thrift stores,
5. Providing senior citizens housing, or
6. Deriving portfolio income from capital asset sales.

Yet there are certain activities that have been excluded from unrelated business income taxation, as follows.

UBI Tax Exceptions from Which a Church Can Benefit

There are ten principle exceptions to the Unrelated Business Income rule of taxation. A church can take advantage of these exceptions to produce income that does not threaten the church's tax-exempt status. The principle exceptions are the following:

1. Deriving investment income
2. Debt financing
3. Conducting publicly traded partnerships
4. Deriving rental income
5. Deriving gains and losses
6. Purchasing options to buy securities
7. Conducting certain types of advertising
8. Hosting bingo
9. Compiling and providing member lists
10. Hosting conventions, fairs, and trade shows

Exception I: Investment Income

In general, all interest, dividends, annuities, and royalties received by the exempt organizations are not taxable. Any income derived from a subsidiary that is more than 80% owned by the exempt organization, however, is taxable as Unrelated Business Income.[24] Income from a church-owned housing complex or day-care facility is likely to be considered UBI.

An important exception to this rule exists: "Unrelated debt-financed income of an exempt organization is taxed as unrelated business income in proportion to the debt existing on the income-producing property."[25] The term "income-producing property" includes real estate as well as financial instruments. Therefore, it would be inappropriate for a church to gain income through leveraged means and expect that income to be tax-exempt. A church should be aware that the manner in which it may obtain portfolio income in the normal course of its operations could determine if it is subject to UBI. As was stated previously, all unrelated business income is nontaxable only to the extent that it is incidental in nature. A church that is simply investing its ready assets in financial instruments cannot be construed as a trade or business outside of the organization's tax-exempt purpose. However, a church that is regularly conducting an investment operation in the manner of a profit-seeking enterprise should be aware that such income is taxable.

Note that it would be prudent for a church to set up a separate corporation in terms of the preceding factors.

Exception II: Debt Financed Income

Debt financed income relates to leveraged property. Such property might include real estate or securities that are held for the production of income. If indebtedness was incurred that related to the income within any of the twelve preceding months, all or a portion of the income may be subject to tax.[26] Any capital gains relating to the disposition of similar property would also be considered UBI.

Any debt-financed property which is held for the production of income is not considered UBI if the use of the property is "substantially related to the exempt purpose of the organization."[27] "Substantially related" means that at least 85% of the use of such property must further the exempt purpose of the organization. If less than 85% of the property is used in relation to the exempt functions of the entity, the non-exempt portion must be considered UBI. Regulation tells us that

1. The portion of time the property is used for exempt purposes is to be compared with the total time it is used for nonexempt purposes, and

2. The portion of the property that is used for exempt purposes is to be compared with the portion of such property that is used for all purposes.[28]

An example of this situation might arise if a church builds a gym with borrowed funds. The gym is considered to be used for one purpose at a time with no annex capable of housing a separate activity. The gym could be rented by the church up to 15% of the time for activities that do not relate to its exempt function. If more than 15% of the time was rented for non-related activities, however, all of the nonrelated income would be considered UBI. In this same example, if the gym was partly financed with borrowed funds and partly with personal funds, an allocation would have to be made between the portion of debt-financed and personal income. The portion of debt-financed income (assuming the 85% limit was breached) will be included in UBI. The personally financed income will be subject to the rules of UBI to determine if tax is due.

In *Gundersen Medical Foundation, Ltd. v. U.S.* 49 AFTRD 2d. 82 (1982), a medical foundation was found to be renting mortgaged property to a clinic. The income from such property was found to be tax-exempt because the operation of the clinic was "substantially related" to the exempt purpose of the foundation.[29] If the clinic's activities had not been so related, the income would have constituted UBI.

In another tax ruling, a tax-exempt organization was taxed on a capital gain realized upon the sale of mortgaged property. The real estate in question was purchased to house administrative functions of the organization. The project did not materialize, thus the building was sold.[30] The ruling in this case suggested that the property was never used in a manner that related to its exempt function. It was, therefore, considered property held for the production of income. The gain on the sale was considered UBI.

There are three principle exceptions to the unrelated debt-financed income rule:

1. Income from property used in excluded research,[31]
2. Property used in a trade or business where substantially all of the labor is provided by volunteers, the activity is carried on for the "convenience of members, students, patients, etc.," or where products sold were donated,[32] and
3. Income from property leased to a medical clinic whose function is related to the exempt purpose of the exempt organization who is serving as the lessor.[33]

Another exception to the debt-financed income rule is that portion of income generated by property used by another related exempt organization. The Internal Revenue Service regulation states that a related organization is

1. One in which one entity "is an exempt holding company,"
2. One organization which has control of the other organization,
3. More than 50% of the members of one organization are members of the other, or
4. Each organization is a local organization directly affiliated with a common state, national, or international organization that is also exempt.[34]

There also exists a stipulation for land involving real estate development that is acquired by an exempt organization which is to be used in the future for an exempt related purpose. This is known as the "neighborhood land rule." The "neighborhood land rule" states that in situations involving *churches only*, debt-financed property will not be considered debt-financed property for a period of up to 15 years. In order to qualify for this, the property must be held with the express intent to use it for the exempt function of the church within the 15 years.

If the property is disposed of within this time period, it still will not be considered debt-financed. The church must, after the first five years, satisfy the Internal Revenue Service that the property is actually being held with the intent of being used for the exempt purpose of the church. "Proof of intent" must include a definite plan complete with dates of exempt conversion, and progress toward such a goal must be shown. This plan must be forwarded to the Internal Revenue Service not less than 90 days before the end of the fifth year after the debt-financed property was acquired.[35]

For example, in a tax ruling, a church proposed to construct a parking lot with borrowed funds. The lot was to be rented outside of the exempt purpose of the church for a period until the rental income had satisfied the debt. It was then to be used for the exempt function. This time period took place in less than 15 years. The Internal Revenue Service ruled that this plan was acceptable.

Exception III: Publicly Traded Partnership

Publicly traded partnerships are traded on an established securities market and are readily tradable in a secondary market.[36] All income from such an activity is considered unrelated business income to a tax-exempt entity. Therefore, the partner's share of income, less any normally allowable deductions, will be included in taxable income.

Exception IV: Rents Received

Rents received from real property are excludable from UBI. There are three exceptions to this exclusion:

1. Debt-financed property which relates to income-producing property (rental income from such property is taxable);
2. Rent received from real property that is leased with personal property. If 50% or more of the rent received from such leased property is personal in nature, it is taxable. Furthermore, the aggregate rents from all such property must be considered "incidental" in nature. The term "incidental" is described as 10% or less of all the rental property combined.[37] This situation could arise if a church had obtained leased personal property and then rented that same property of which such rents would be taxable;
3. Rentals based upon a percentage of the net income derived from property will be considered taxable. If a church rented commercial property, and the amount of rent owed was based upon a percentage of the income from such property, the income would be taxable.

Exception V: Gains and Losses

Any gain or loss from the sale or exchange of property is excluded from tax. The exceptions:

1. "The cutting of timber that is treated as a sale or exchange,"
2. "Debt-financed property,"
3. "Property that can be classified as inventory," and
4. "Property held primarily for sale in the ordinary course of business."[38]

Exception VI: Options to Buy Securities

Any gain realized from the termination of an option to buy or sell securities is not included in UBI. "An option is considered terminated when the organization's obligation under the option ceases by any means other than by reason of the exercise or lapse of the option."[39]

Exception VII: Certain Advertising Activities

In general, income generated for advertising is considered unrelated business income. Specifically, advertising that is designed to support the organization's exempt purpose is not taxable. For example, income derived by a church from advertising church sponsored activities may be considered unrelated business income. If an advertisement for a product or service was also included in the publication, the portion of that income will be considered unrelated business income.

Conventions and trade shows are considered exempt income if the purpose of the activity is to enhance the organization's exempt function. If the primary purpose of the activity is to sell a product or service unrelated to the exempt function, all income will be considered taxable.[40]

Income received from advertising in a tax-exempt publication is considered an "exploitation of the organization's exempt activities."[41] In other words, the fact that the issuing organization operates under an exempt status does not justify unrelated advertising in its literature. Each case must be considered in using the general rules stated above.

For example, in *Florida Trucking Association Inc.*, 87 TC 1039, an exempt organization received income from advertising that was published in the entity's newsletter.[42] The advertisements were not related to the exempt purpose of the organization. Therefore, all income related to these advertisements was considered UBI. In another case, *Fraternal Order of Police, Illinois State Troopers Lodge No. 41 v. Commissioner,* 60 AFTRD 2d (1987), a magazine was issued by the taxpayer containing a listing of nonrelated business services and products. The court found that these advertisements constituted UBI.[43] Churches should keep in mind that not all advertising is considered UBI.

In *U.S. v. American College of Physicians,* 57 AFTRD 86 (1986), advertisements that were related to the contents of the magazine were considered consistent with the exempt purpose of the organization; therefore, the income was not considered UBI.[44] The factors used to determine whether advertising income is UBI lie within the relation to the exempt purpose of the organization. Furthermore, the advertisements must meet the other tests of UBI, such as the regular operation of a trade or business.

Exception VIII: Bingo

Income from Bingo games are exempt if the games comply with local laws and do not constitute unfair competition with profit-seeking entities.[45] Local laws are key in this area. If the local law allows exempt bingo in specified areas, income is not taxable. Furthermore, if all the work is carried on by volunteers, income is not considered UBI.[46]

In *Waco Lodge No. 166, B.P.O.E. v Commissioner,* 51 AFTRD 629 (1983), proceeds from the conduct of bingo games were considered UBI when the games are illegal under state law and a large percentage of the workers are paid.[47] The Waco Lodge may have avoided paying tax if local law had allowed the games or a substantial amount of the labor had been provided by volunteers.

In another case, income from a weekly bingo game was not considered UBI. The state considered the games illegal, but the local government considered the games legal. The games were not in competition on a commercial basis.[48] In another tax ruling, the fact that an organization compensated a professional bingo promoter did not make the proceeds from the game UBI. The games were legal under the local law and did not compete with a for-profit enterprise.[49]

Exception IX: Member Lists

Income derived from the exchange of lists between two tax-exempt entities is non-taxable.[50]

Exception X: Conventions, Fairs, and Trade Shows

Income-producing activities that are in conjunction with an "international, national, or local fair or exposition" are not considered UBI.[51] There is an important qualification in this area. The fair must be both educational and agricultural in nature. It must also be regularly conducted as one of the exempt purposes of the organization. This qualification would rule these events out for most churches.

Conventions must be conducted with the intent of educating "its members . . . promoting and stimulating interest in and a demand for the products or services of the industry's members."[52] Therefore, income produced from a church-related convention is not considered UBI. The convention must attempt to obtain its purpose through a "significant portion of the exhibits or the character of conferences and seminars held at the convention or meeting."[53]

Income from the rental of space at such a convention is not considered UBI. This is true even if the space is being used for the sale of products or services. It should be remembered that the majority of the exhibits of such an event must be related to the exempt function of the sponsoring organization.

The exceptions listed above give church organizations a wide degree of freedom in their fund-raising activities. The help of a tax attorney should be obtained to structure transactions prudently or to determine if a church may benefit from these exceptions. Determinations of whether a church can benefit from the exceptions and to what extent it may benefit entails very technical arrangements which a church should not attempt on its own.

With the guidance of a tax attorney and careful planning, a church can produce income without jeopardizing its tax-exempt status.

TAX GUIDELINES FOR MINISTERS AND CHURCHES

In the ordinary course of business, churches normally compensate ministers and staff personnel that perform services for the organization. Certain compensation may be exempt for income for those personnel, but excessive compensation can cause the government to revoke an organization's exempt status.

Following are a few rules which will help a church to be successful in avoiding tax problems. The IRS uses the term "minister" to mean a particular person. A minister is "one who is a duly ordained, commissioned, or licensed minister of a church."[54] The minister must perform activities within the church that qualify him as a practicing minister. He must perform religious services or functions that would be considered duties of a minister within that particular church. A minister must be a practicing staff member to be considered a minister for tax purposes. A minister does not necessarily have to be working within a church building. These facts are important because ministers are subject to special income and tax-exemptions.

Generally, any fees regarding salaries or wages, marriage, counseling, funeral, or special speaking engagements are taxable to a minister. However, any allowance or provision made to house a minister is exempt from taxable income and is excluded from the gross income. This includes

1. Rentals
2. Housing allowances
3. Furniture, fixtures, and appliance allowances
4. Cost of home improvements
5. Insurance
6. Maintenance and repairs
7. Mortgage payments made by the church

Regulations tell us that any expenses incurred by rent or purchase or otherwise related to "providing a home," including utilities, are tax-exempt.[55] This exemption cannot exceed reasonable compensation. Reasonable compensation is an amount that would be necessary in similar circumstances. Excessive compensation paid out can cause problems for the church.

A good example of the problems of excessive compensation can be seen in the case involving the Reverend Jim Bakker. His compensation was excessive and was cited as being over 1.6 million dollars in 1986. Reasonable compensation is the amount that would ordinarily be paid for like services by like organizations under like circumstances.[56] The Commissioner questioned the issue of whether or not the PTL was an exempt organization. In the future, the decision of this case may be used as a standard for all exempt organizations. The courts found that parts of the PTL's earnings were unreasonable compensation. In reality the PTL's earnings were inuring to the benefit of Bakker, and therefore considered non-exempt. The government revoked the PTL's exempt status and all its earnings were taxable for the years during which the inurement took place. A considerable amount of back taxes, along with penalties and interest, were due. Bakker was found guilty of fraud and tax evasion and was sentenced to federal prison.

To receive a parsonage allowance exclusion a cleric must satisfy both the definition of minister and accept rent-free use of a house or a housing allowance. This housing exclusion does not include things such as food, personal toiletries, or servants.

The boundaries of this rule were tested in a 1984 case involving James L. Swaggart and his church. Mr. Swaggart was qualified as an ordained minister, but he provided a home for himself. This home was "free from any mortgage indebtedness," yet he received a rental allowance from his church. The court found that the allowance was not excludable from being taxable income because "such rental allowance was not used to rent a home, make payments towards the purchase of a home, nor used for any additional items associated with providing a home."[57]

Ministers have a double tax benefit in the housing exemption area. They can deduct mortgage interest or real property taxes on their individual tax return. This benefit was provided by the Tax Reform Act of 1986 which overruled an earlier position taken by the IRS in 1982 in which a minister could not claim these deductions.

Non-ministerial employees can also qualify for parsonage exclusion if their housing is

1. Furnished on their employer's business premises,
2. For their employer's convenience, and
3. As a condition of their employment.

All three of these conditions must be met in order for the housing for a non-ministerial to be non-taxable.[58]

It is important that a church develop a budget based upon estimated costs and needs of its ministerial staff. This could help prevent problems of overspending. The church should also keep records of the amount of funds available and how they are spent on the minister's income and parsonage. Failure to maintain funds according to the organization's exempt status can result in severe hardship for its workers, as well as for itself. Exemption revocations can be declared on a retroactive basis. This could result in excessive back taxes, penalties, and interest.

Church organizations should be aware of pitfalls when they assign compensation to their workers. Ministers can avoid a confrontation with the IRS if they are careful to exclude only that income which is used for and related to providing a dwelling place. Furthermore, excessive compensation paid to a minister can cause a revocation of the organization's exempt status and will hurt that individual. Churches also need to keep records for tax purposes, of who is an employee, ministerial and non-ministerial staff.

Individual Inurement Effects on Tax Liability

Theoretically, churches and nonprofit tax-exempt organizations are not supposed to benefit any one person. If a church is deemed to be operating for the benefit of one person, it can lose its tax-exempt status. Sometimes a person can be considered a minister by definition of duties, but the organization can be considered nonexempt because of the inurement of benefits to a single individual.[59] This inurement rule only effects tax-exempt organizations. If a religious organization is deemed to be nonexempt, then the church staff and/or the minister may be liable for back taxes, penalties, and any applicable interest.

The court revoked the tax-exempt status for the Church of Scientology of California on the grounds that wealth accumulation of the church was inuring to its founder L. Ron Hubbard. It was ruled that Hubbard was receiving benefit from the organization's income by receiving proceeds that amounted to 10% of the gross income of its various congregations. He also was found to be collecting royalties from copyrighted works that were produced by the organization's members. Finally, Mr. Hubbard had "unfettered control over millions of dollars in Church assets," with an absence of formal records or means of documentation to record the use of these funds. Mr. Hubbard was therefore liable for back taxes, penalties, and interest.[60]

There have been other cases like the Scientology case across the country. One case involved an "Illinois Not-For-Profit Corporation" called Easter House. Its primary exempt function was to operate as an adoption agency. This agency was found to actually be operating like a commercial organization and accumulated a substantial capital surplus.[61] Net profits were inured to the benefit of a private individual who received an excessive salary. The agency was also found to be making loans to separate organizations that were owned by or were employers of the same individuals. Easter House's tax-exempt status was revoked.

The mere fact that an organization is accumulating wealth does not mean that this wealth is necessarily inuring for the benefit of one individual. In regards to the Presbyterian and Reformed Publishing suit, the court held that an organization's exempt status should be reinstated because substantial profits did not inure to the benefit of one individual. In this case a select group of employees received modest salaries (under $16,000). In 1980, a lower court found this to be inurement to one individual. Exempt status for the organization was revoked. The decision became retroactive for "January 1, 1969 onward." The appellate court ruled that the payments were not excessive in nature and did not represent "private inurement."[62]

It is important to note that the definition of inurement may be different in each case. The fact that no individual may receive a substantial salary does not effect the idea of inurement. The income must be considered reasonable payment for services rendered. A small salary may be considered inurement if the payment is considered unreasonable.

Who Must File a Tax Return, and Record Keeping

Churches and ministers must be aware of who must file a tax return in order to avoid problems. The Internal Revenue Service determines who must file an income tax return based upon the individual's gross income earned. There are seven main categories in which an individual may fit. They are:

1. Single person (under 65) . . . gross income $**
   (**must be checked each year depending on tax law changes),
2. Single person (65 and over . . . gross income $** (above),
3. Married, filing joint returns (under 65) . . . gross income $ . . .
4. Married, filing joint returns (1 spouse 65 or over) . . . gross income level $ . . ., and
5. Married, filing joint returns (both spouses over 65) . . . gross income $...[63]

Even if a church minister or employee does not fit within one of these categories they must file a return if they are self-employed. Practically all individual tax returns must be mailed by April 15. Extensions, however, can be obtained by contacting the Internal Revenue Service.

A minister or church must keep track of any documents such as receipts or canceled checks which relate to their return. These documents and a copy of the filed return should be kept at least four years after filing it or after the date the tax is paid, whichever is later. Payroll records should also be maintained and saved. This is a precaution to protect the church and minister if they are audited, and the church must substantiate their expenses.

Self-Employed and Employed Ministers' Federal Income Taxes

The employment status of a minister determines which standard one must follow in filing federal income tax returns. A minister can be considered employed or self-employed. Self-employed ministers file differently than employed ministers. The distinction between the two types of ministers hinges upon the "common law" definition of an employee. The church is the minister's employer if the church has

1. The right to control (in a working sense) an individual who is performing tasks in his or her behalf,
2. The authority to dismiss an individual from services,
3. The power to provide tools for use in service, and
4. The authority to determine the location of the service.

The minister is an employee, according to the IRS, when the above factors are present. These same standards exist for non-ministerial employees. The distinction between employed and self-employed ministers is very important. The IRS uses the distinction

1. To determine where on the tax returns the cleric deducts business expenses,
2. To determine which form and where income should be reported,
3. To determine whether certain fringe benefits are excludable from the minister's income or should be reported, and
4. To decide whether a church can provide the employee with a qualified retirement plan or tax-sheltered annuity. Self-employed individuals must supply their own separate qualified retirement plan.[64]

A church is not required to withhold taxes from an ordained minister's pay. Such a withholding consideration is optional.[65]

A church official or minister should always contact a tax advisor before making these types of determinations. A church must withhold both federal and social security taxes (unless they are exempted) from a minister's pay.

Social Security Tax

Social Security taxes must be paid on income received from the church. These taxes are paid both by the individual and the church[66] and must be withheld on a timely basis. There are two distinct types of social security tax. They are FICA (Federal Insurance Contribution Act) and SECA (Self-Employment Contributions Act). Each type of tax has a different set of rules that apply. Likewise, there are two different degrees of employees, non-minister and minister. There are a different set of rules governing each of them. Interestingly, if a minister is deemed ineligible for the parsonage exclusion, then they will usually be considered an employee and subject to FICA tax.

Ministerial Employee Social Security Tax

A church must remember that the standards used to determine federal tax status do not apply to determinations concerning social security tax. For Social Security purposes all ministers are considered self-employed. This is true even if a minister is considered an employee for federal income tax purposes. Therefore, churches must make SECA withholdings from the minister's pay. A minister is not responsible for paying FICA taxes, because no person is subject to both types of taxes. Income under $400, however, is not subject to the SECA tax.[67]

A minister can attempt to avoid paying the SECA tax by filing form 4361. This form allows a minister who takes a vow of poverty to apply for SECA tax-exemption on the grounds that he or she is opposed to the insurance plan because of "conscientious" reasons or because of "religious principles." Proper credentials must be presented to qualify for this exemption. The Internal Revenue Service will not allow such an exemption on "economic grounds."[68] The IRS must be convinced that the applicant truly does oppose the plan on "conscientious" or "religious grounds." Form 4361 must be filled out properly to qualify. Ministers must follow the directions carefully. Any mistakes or missing information will cause the request to be denied.

SECA taxes can be paid in a variety of manners. Ministers can make regular payments based upon an estimate of taxes due or pay all at once. The amount of SECA tax is found by multiplying the net earnings from self-employment by the applicable self-employment tax rate. Net earnings from self-employment generally consists of gross income from self-employment less allowable deductions attributable to such income.[69] Items such as pension and annuity plans should not be considered a part of gross income.

Non-Ministerial Employee Social Security Tax

Non-minister personnel includes all workers who are considered employees "under the usual common law rules applicable in determining employer-employee relationship(s)."[70] If a person is an employee of a church, FICA taxes must be withheld from the employee's pay. All income which is not for ministerial capacities is subject to FICA. The church must match FICA taxes paid by the employee.[71]

It is very important that churches pay close attention to these payments. Failure to make such payments could result in the church becoming liable for the tax. If a church is found negligent in employee withholding payments and the individual is exempt or that the employee requested that no tax be withheld, the church may become liable for those taxes.[72]

At times it can be difficult to determine whether or not an individual is or is not an employee of the church. Part-time workers and incidental employees or agents make this determination even more unclear. Independent contractors are not considered employees of the church.[73] This includes contractors, lawyers, and other individuals who operate a separate "trade or business." Churches should be fully aware of whether or not individuals are serving them as employees.

Failure to withhold FICA taxes could result in the church assuming the debt. FICA tax does not necessarily have to be withheld for employees

1. Who earn less than a certain amount during a calendar year,[74]
2. Who are non-immigrant employees who possess an F or J visa,[75]
3. In foreign countries who are subject to foreign Social Security Taxes (they may be exempt under an international agreement),[76]
4. Who elect not to be subject to FICA taxation (This is done by filing form 8274. The employees would then be subject to SECA taxation.), and
5. Who are students.[77]

If a church is unclear as to how much tax to withhold and what type, it should contact a tax specialist or tax accountant.

Discrimination

An organization can lose its tax-exempt status through the practice of discrimination. Some organizations are even required to file, each year, a certificate stating that they do not discriminate. Therefore, it is very important that churches take careful measures not to discriminate against individuals by sex, race, age, or other factors or criteria that shall be examined herein.

Title VII of the 1964 Civil Rights Act states that

1. It shall be an unlawful employment practice for an employer:
   a. To fail or refuse to hire or discharge any individual, or otherwise to discriminate against any individual with respect to his compensation, terms, conditions, or privileges of employment,

because of such individual's race, color, religion, sex, or national origin;

b. To limit, segregate, or classify his employees or applicants for employment in any way which would deprive or tend to deprive any individual of employment opportunities or otherwise adversely affect his status as an employee, because of such individual's race, color, religion, sex, or national origin.

Title VII only applies to "employers who employ 15 or more persons, for each working day in each of 20 or more calendar weeks in the current or preceding year."[78] Many church organizations do not meet this requirement.

Title VII also applies to religious sponsored schools and universities. In the case of *Bob Jones University v United States*, it was proven that a tax-exempt organization could lose its exempt status for the practice of racial discrimination.[79] Therefore, from a taxation standpoint, it is very important that an organization refrain from any form of discrimination.

The 1963 Equal Pay Act requires that men and women receive equal pay for "equal skill, effort, and responsibility." This rule is part of the Fair Labor Standards Act. There are no specific exceptions to this rule. Willful violation of this rule could result in the payment of twice the amount of damages that were actually incurred. With this in mind, churches should make sure that they practice a method of equal payment for equal work among all its employees.

Conclusion

Church organizations have a tremendous privilege in the form of tax-exemption. Yet, there are a variety of rules that govern this area. It is very important that each minister and church makes itself aware of these rules and regulations. Failure to obtain such knowledge could result in a violation that may require unnecessary penalties or the loss of tax-exemption all together. A tax attorney should always be consulted to avoid potential tax problems.

4

Marketing Religion with Today's Technology

When the student is ready, the doors to life will open!
There is always something better....
If we open ourselves, there is no limit with the infinite [power].

TELEVISION OR RADIO: WHICH TO CHOOSE?

There are many things to consider when deciding to broadcast a religious program on television or radio. One of the key issues to consider is how to market the program. Marketing religion on television or radio raises these questions:

1. How does one get started?
2. How should one organize?
3. How much will it cost?

Other issues revolve around what messages the church wants to convey and how it should convey them.

A church can use either radio or television to air a program. Both mediums have a lot in common and both are effective forms of mass communications which churches can use to convey their messages. The relationships of churches between radio and television stations are very similar, but the two mediums do have their differences. Unlike television, radio is a very mobile and flexible form of communication. Most people have at least one radio in their cars, homes, or offices. This mobility allows radio to convey its messages to diverse audiences all at once. Changes in recent years have been made to make televisions smaller to compete with radio in terms of mobility, but television has yet to achieve the mobility of radio.

Today, television offers an opportunity to reach a larger and more diverse audience than radio. There is, however, also a cost difference between the two mediums. Radio tends to be a less expensive medium than television. This includes production costs as well as the costs of air time. The following will help to guide the church through the process of developing a radio or television program while offering helpful advice on how to accomplish its goals.

Target Audiences

Radio and television are powerful communication mediums. They can be used by a church to pass on its message without many complications and attract members that it normally would not attract. The process of creating and maintaining a religious program on radio or television is very similar. Whether a church chooses to use radio or television depends upon its message, target audience, and budget. A national radio or television program would increase the programs target audience but at higher costs. Local air time would target smaller, more specific audiences at lower costs.

Careful planning and preparation must be executed before a church can create a religious program. Preparation is key to the church's media success. The church must decide

1. Who its target audience will be,
2. What message it wants to convey to the audience,
3. How this message will be conveyed.

Traditionally, radio and television church programs have targeted home-bound audiences and other people who were unable to physically attend church services. The programs were mainly the same services as those provided by the church. Progressive churches should not limit themselves to these types of programs. It is reasonably believed that "the more varied and less obviously religious a radio program is," the less likely it is that a listener will turn it off.[80] The format that a church chooses is key to the conveyance of its message.

Formats of Television and Radio

Format is key to successful religious programming. The format is simply what style the church will use for presentation. An important format decision is the choice of who the speaker or commentator of the program will be. Listeners and viewers have a tendency to be loyal to a particular speaker rather than a particular faith.[81]

Choosing the right person to lead the program could immensely expand a church's potential audience. A charismatic television or radio leader should be trained both in religion and broadcasting. The audience must be able to connect with the program's leader and content to make them want to view or listen again. The audience's response to a program and its leader can either generate more funds for the program or kill it by reducing the contributions that it receives.

Since contact with the audience is so important, many churches initiate programs to please the viewers and listeners. Churches must never forget the needs and the power of their audiences, whether they are using television or radio to express their beliefs.

A church must alter its services to fit the basic formats of radio and television. Because television is extremely visual in most cases, the church's religious program should be different from the services performed in the church. The service should be changed to include more movement using graphics and the use of different lighting techniques or camera shots. These additions could be used to keep the viewers' attention.

If radio is the medium that the church chooses to use, the program must be adapted to fit the formats of radio. Unlike television, the programming on radio stations is very specific, and it thrives upon its consistency. Radio stations attempt to give an audience a specialized format throughout the day.

Television viewers have several stations and program options from which to choose. The church's program must have a special quality presentation to compel viewers to watch. Television has a wide variety of formats in which this can be done. A church can use drama, comedy, sermons, music, or talk format to build a successful and enjoyable show. Religious programming needs to be religious and inspirational with a tinge of entertainment to be successful—this is true of television and radio.[82]

The church must make sure that its program's format is appropriately adapted to the programming style of the broadcasting station. The program format must compliment the format of the station. If it is inconsistent, then the church will lose potential audience listeners who will simply turn to another station. Radio formats include those used of television, but there is no visual demand. The church must use sound to keep the listener's attention. If a church has a choir, this would be a great opportunity to use music to capture an audience. These are all things which a church must consider when developing radio programs. A church, however, can successfully use both radio and television to express its opinions.

Sustaining Time

Since the birth of television and radio, the government has regulated their usage and the allotment of frequencies. Today, many regulations have been eliminated or relaxed. One regulation that was relaxed required that television and radio stations provide free air time for organizations to use, "in the public interest, convenience, or necessity."[83] Television and radio stations were required to air programs of public interest in order to have their licenses renewed. Religious programming was one of the many programs available to fill these time slots and express public interests.

This free public interest air time was called "sustaining time." Sustaining time was available to any church or organization who wished to use it. But fierce competition among television and radio stations to make money quickly changed the availability of "sustaining time." Stations realized that they could make profits by selling the air time that was once offered free of charge to programmers and churches who were willing to pay for it. This enabled the stations to make money while simultaneously satisfying the Federal Communications Commission's (FCC) requirements for airing public interest programming.

The trend in offering churches more paid time and less sustaining time" has a profound effect upon how churches operated in the media. The religious television and radio programs that were aired became limited to those churches who could afford the cost of buying air time. Smaller and less affluent churches began to disappear from the media. Because of this, the diversity of styles and denominations of religious television and radio programs began to disappear.

Where Churches Can Broadcast

Churches are limited to the available areas of broadcasting for television. There are three basic television areas available to churches who wish to broadcast on television:

1. The networks and their local affiliates
2. UHF stations
3. Cable stations

National paid time for television is the most expensive of the three choices. A half-hour time block on Sunday at 5:00 A.M. in one major city can cost $3,000. Those churches that have been economically pressured from the networks can use the UHF frequencies, which are less expensive. UHF's expansion also offers opportunities for churches to purchase their own television stations.

Cable television is also an option for churches. Unlike basic television stations, cable companies have different requirements regarding public interest programming. Most "cable companies do not have to provide access channels unless they are negotiated in the contract—the franchise between the community and the cable company."[84] Therefore, access requirements for cable channels vary from community to community. Cable access is a good place for churches to start experimenting with their programming. Cable companies usually offer free training sessions for camera operation and editing techniques.

In contrast, radio offers slightly different choices for churches. Churches who wish to broadcast on radio have two options as to where they can broadcast from: national syndication or local stations. The strategies to use each of them are varied. Today most religious radio programs are done locally due to the high cost of national air time.

Local programming is also more popular because it offers the church more control over when and where their programs are broadcast. This helps the church to better reach its target audience. Churches have a better chance of receiving use of this free sustaining time from local stations than they have from a national station.

Local programming, however, does have a disadvantage. Churches which use local public service sustaining time, "may be subjected to various restrictions under the guise of station policy."[85] These rules and regulations are normally targeted to censor or limit the content of the church's program.

Though it is costly, national air time is a viable option for churches. There are several well-known national programs which are in syndication today. Churches must keep in mind that most national programs are aired because the church purchased the air time from the radio station. The cost of buying this air time can be very expensive.

Economics of Television and Radio

The consideration of expense relative to television and radio programming is very important. Religious programs on both radio and television are usually aired early on Sunday mornings or late at night. These are normally the cheapest air times offered because the audiences awake at those hours are limited. Churches can contact their local radio and television stations sales departments to inquire about rates.

There is one major disadvantage to using paid time for religious programs on radio and television. These programs are usually extremely dependent upon their viewing audience for financial support. Direct contact with the audience is key to a paid time program. Television viewers tend to give more contributions than do congregation members that attend services in the church or non-viewers.[86] Radio programs have experienced similar reactions from its listeners.

These contributions from the public allow the church to buy air time on television and radio which in turn funds other church activities and services. Any dramatic reduction in these contributions could force a program off the air. For this reason, some believe that paid time programs have "sacrificed that freedom of programming when they made themselves dependent on their popularity with their television audience."[87] Churches which use the sustaining time do not have this pressure. Theoretically, they have more freedom in the presentation and content of their program, on both television and radio.

Limitations of Television and Radio

Radio and television, like all other forms of communications, have their limits and churches must keep these in mind. Television is a very expensive means of communication. Because of this cost, many novice broadcasters are either intimidated by the cost of television or cannot afford to use it. For radio, "any station, even a 50,000-watt clear channel outlet, is limited in the audience it can attract."[88] Radio stations also compete with television and other radio stations which may be targeting the same audience. There is increasing competition among television networks and cable stations. Churches can use the competitive atmosphere of television and radio to their advantage by shopping around for the lowest possible prices. Stations can occasionally be persuaded to lower their prices if another station is doing the same.

Conclusion

Radio and television religious programming demands a lot from churches. Churches must be prepared to make major decisions and conduct a lot of planning. One of the first decisions to be made by a church will be whether to use radio or television as a means to broadcast its program. The broader audience of television makes it a very attractive option for churches. But the less expensive radio air time and its specialized audience can help a church to convey its message to those it wants to attract at a cheaper rate.

The economics of mass-media production cannot be ignored by churches. The advantages and disadvantages of national versus local air time on each medium must also be considered, for the whole purpose of the program is to reach a certain audience.

The choice of what program format to use must also be made by the church. A church must decide which of these choices will facilitate achievement of projected goals. These decisions should not be made lightly. Successful usage of radio and television can add members to a congregation or bring new life to the existing congregation. A church can move into a progressive stage of growth and be more effective in its ministry by utilizing radio and television to convey its message.

GOSPEL MUSIC RECORDING

The gospel music industry is growing and producing many opportunities for progressive churches. In the late 1980's, gospel music changed direction. Gospel groups and singers, such as Tremaine Hawkins, the Winans, and Amy Grant began to have success on the pop charts. These crossover artists increased the appeal of gospel music to the general public.

Church members have two principle ways to gain entry into the gospel music industry. A church can record a demo tape for use in trying to solicit a major record deal, or a church can record, press, and market its own product. Attempting to acquire a major record deal using a demo tape can be a trying process, but beneficial. Independently recording and marketing the music are the most expensive methods, but with work, it can be extremely rewarding and successful. The church's organizational skills, goals, and costs that it can absorb will determine which method is best suited for the church. There are a few basic rules that a church attempting either method may follow.

A gospel group seeking to obtain a major recording deal and make its own records must have a plan or strategy. This strategy is purely organizational and must begin with a budget. The church must also decide who will perform on the album. This can include soloists, groups or choirs, and musicians. Once the group has been chosen, they should rehearse their songs and find the best 3–4 songs and concentrate on perfecting them. These songs will comprise the demo tape. Rehearsals are imperative to avoid expensive re-takes and later problems.

A demo tape is the gospel group's key to open the doors for a recording deal. A demo tape is a selection of 3–4 songs (no more than 4) which showcases the performer's vocal abilities. The group's vocal abilities should be the focal point as opposed to the music. The songs to be recorded should be well rehearsed before a gospel group enters a recording studio. Recording studios usually charge by the hour making any extensive rehearsal time at the studio very costly for most churches, as well as for secular enterprises.

A professional studio can make creating a demo tape easier for a church. Churches should call around to price recording studios. Some studios charge under $100, but some charge several hundred dollars an hour. There are studios that will even negotiate their prices depending on the project. The church should ask if the performers can watch others recording so that they can get a feel for studio recording and learn from others' mistakes.

The studio should have up-to-date equipment, which should include dubbing capabilities. An ill-equipped studio will limit the artistic quality of the production and the artist's ability to showcase his or her talents. If the church does not have someone who knows how to operate the recording equipment, the studio may provide a studio engineer. The studio should provide an engineer who will aid in recording, mixing, and other technical duties. The engineer can add the finishing touches to a recording which will enhance the quality of the recording. It is from this recording that the group makes its demo tapes.

The church group should also choose someone in its organization to educate himself on studio language, equipment, techniques, and etiquette. This person can help others, even though they may not be able to run the equipment. This can also minimize reproduction problems and help assure a quality recording. Preparation and professionalism in the studio will help the recording session to be expedient and efficient.

Approaching a Record Company

The next step is approaching a record label. The group should target those companies which have shown an interest in gospel music. A representative for the gospel group should contact prospective record labels to try to get an audition for a demo tape that could possibly lead to a recording contract. At this stage in the process, the group may wish to get an agent or an entertainment attorney. A key factor is being linked to someone who has gospel music connections and inside know-how to increase the group's chances for success. The group's representative should contact the record company to find out the name, telephone number, and address of a contact person to whom they should send their demo tape. The label representative should be contacted in advance to inform him that the demo tape is being forwarded. Sending demo tapes without notice will almost always guarantee that the demo tape will not be heard.

The promotional package that a group or artist will send must contain the following:

1. Demo tape cassette (preferably 4 recordings)
2. Photographs
3. Biographical information (a short sketch of each artist)
4. Video cassette if possible

The recordings should be labeled with the artist's or group's name, address, phone number, titles of the songs, and length of each song. The group should make sure that this labeling is secure. It would be very frustrating for record label representatives to develop interest only to find that they are unable to contact the performers.

Additionally, the package should contain a credit sheet (indicating who worked on the recording), a copy of the lyrics to each song, and any press coverage on the artists. The group should make as many copies of these packages as it intends to send the record companies. All of these things make it easier for the record label to make an informed judgment. Record company representatives listen to several demo tapes a day. Making things as convenient for them as possible can only help the artist or group gain favor.

The record label representative should be contacted again 10–14 days after the package is sent. This contact is to ensure that the demo tape arrived and to get an appraisal of the work. If your demo tape was reviewed, the church representative should then politely ask for an assessment of the material. It is at this point that the company will generally offer a deal, an opportunity to record more (or further analysis), or express disinterest. Whether the news is good or bad, hearing the representative's critique of the recording can help the artist avoid mistakes and improve future recordings.

A church gospel group needs to retain the services of an entertainment attorney before any contracts or agreements are negotiated or signed to ensure that the gospel group obtains the most advantageous contract without endangering the church's exempt status.

It is at this stage that the method of releasing and recording the product deviates from the first (demo) method. The independent record producer enters the recording studio with the same problems—seeking to obtain a deal from a major record label. The main exception is that the independent record producer wants to make a master copy of the songs recorded (usually four) and may not want a record deal. Records, cassettes, and CDs will be produced from this master copy. The independent producer has the extra burden of finding a place to produce these media. Facilities must be modern to ensure clarity of recording and quality of sound. Any distortions in the pressing stage will be amplified when the recording is played.

Once the product has been made, the independent record producer must market and sell the recording. Radio airplay and exposure can make a record a success. A radio station's programmer or director should be approached to try to get the product added to the play list. This can be a hard sale to make. Many stations play only what is on the pop and R&B charts or the charts linked to their station's formats. If the station has a new music or local talent program, that program format can be used to showcase the record. Getting people to listen to the record is essential in encouraging the general public to buy the recording. Many times small local record stores are more hesitant to sell independently produced work.

Because there is no major record label to market the record and encourage sales, the responsibilities fall on the shoulders of the producer. This method can be difficult and expensive, but it can be successful. If the producer has a record which does well, all the profits can go to him and the church. There are no middlemen to take away from the return. Thus, the work is hard, but the rewards can be tremendous.

Publishing

Churches can publish both the songs they record and others. Operating a publishing company would give churches the power to own and control the songs and their usage. Entering the publishing business is not as difficult as some church organizers may believe. Once the church has the songs that it wishes to record, it should enter into an agreement with the songwriters. These agreements should stipulate who controls the usage of the songs, distribution of the songs, and how publishing royalties will be regulated. Churches should not attempt to develop such an agreement without the aid of an attorney to avoid potential problems.

After this has been done, the church should copyright the songs. Copyrighting the material will give the church present and future legal control over the songs. Since copyrighting is a legal procedure, the church should solicit the aid of an attorney. Copyright requests must be made using specific governmental forms. Mistakes or failure to disclose information will lead to a denial of the copyright request.

If the copyright is granted, then a church is on its way to building a publishing company. The church should seek out a printing company which can print the material when needed. The songs must then be marketed in order to generate income. Record labels, independent artists or even people affiliated with the church may want to use the songs. The church can generate revenue by requiring that these people pay for the song usage and even obtaining a percentage of any residuals from the song sales. Operating a publishing company can allow a church to control more of its own recording efforts. The financial benefits of owning the copyright is unlimited.

The church should consider establishing a separate corporation to carry out recording or publishing activities to avoid jeopardizing the church's tax exempt status.

Conclusion

The gospel music industry can provide a progressive church with a great opportunity to showcase the talents of its congregation and spread its message. There are two basic methods for recording a successful record. The church's group can make a demo tape and try to get a recording contract with an established label, or it can produce the record itself. There are some common characteristics between the two methods, most notably, both require money. Producing a demo tape or record can be very expensive. A church should establish a budget of how much it is willing and able to spend on the production. Having a budget will keep the expense of recording from growing beyond a church's means. The church's group must select the talent to use and a studio in which to record its demo tape. These two selections are key to a good recording.

What happens after recording the demo tape depends on the method that a church group follows. If the group tries to gain a record deal from a label, then it must contact the label and then present their demo tape to showcase their talents. If a record company likes the demo tape, it can spell success for a group. In contrast, an independent producer will make a master copy of the work in the studio and produce a record, cassette, or CD from this master. A lot of music industry knowledge is required to implement this method. The hardest part of being an independent producer is marketing the product and getting airtime on the radio. Once the public learns of the record and buys it, the independent producer can become a success. The amount of money and industry knowledge that a church group has will determine which method it uses. A church can use either method to enter the gospel music industry.

A church should solicit the help of an entertainment attorney before any contracts are signed and secure an appraisal of its tax situation. Careful planning is required to ensure that churches do not lose their tax-exempt status and that the most advantageous record deal possible is secured.

5

Fund-Raising Techniques

Mistakes are necessary when they occur for growth.
One who is resistant to new ideas cannot grow.

When it comes to fund-raising, churches have many techniques and options available. Churches may use capital campaigns, memorial gifts, tithe contributions, or several other techniques to accomplish their goals. The goals and purpose of the church are important, because they will guide how a fund-raising venture will be carried out. Planning, research, and strong marketing skills can be used to fulfill the church's goals both religiously and economically. The needs of the church's potential donor also cannot be ignored when operating a fund-raising program. There are several approaches in developing a successful fund-raising program, but the most successful are those which satisfy both the donors' and the church's needs. One of the first steps in planning a fund-raiser is to evaluate the past or current fund-raising techniques.

Evaluating Past Fund-Raising Techniques

A thorough evaluation and overhaul of nonproductive aspects of past efforts can bring new life to a fund-raising campaign. The old cliché, "history repeats itself," does not have to come true if a church learns from its past fund-raising mistakes. The church should consider buying, trading, or sharing donor lists with similar organizations, expanding the potential donor pool of a fund-raiser. Old donor lists should also be revised and updated to reflect changes of addresses and actual donors. Names and addresses of past donors tend to be very useful to churches trying to build a solid fund-raising base. By setting these names and addresses aside, a church can target willing donors, contact lost donors (address changes), and save time and money by not contacting those people who have proven unreceptive. These simple actions will create an opportunity to evaluate why the church's past attempts succeeded or failed.

If past fund-raising techniques have not been successful, a church should try to find out why. Many fund-raising drives fail because of a lack of planning and a flawed requesting approach. Most church donations come from the church's congregation and its surrounding community. Churches must approach these people with certain things in mind. Donation requests should appeal to the donor's emotions, needs, and values. Donors do not give to satisfy an organization's needs, but rather to satisfy something within themselves. A church should show how giving to their organization will fulfill some of the donor's needs. People like to feel as if they are doing their part in helping particular people, animals, and society's needs, not just the church's. If a church can connect the donor's needs with their organizations, their fund-raising efforts will be more profitable.

Traditionally, a church's requests for contributions have merely stated the church's needs. This is a very serious fund-raising mistake. Pleas such as "we need this" or "we're desperate" may encourage one time donations. Most churches need repeat donations to survive over time. The flaw in this type of fund-raising technique is that it does not make the donors feel as if they are benefitting or fulfilling their needs. For instance, since most churches are tax-exempt, contributions to them are tax-deductible. Potential donors should be told this. By simply altering a fund-raising request to reflect how the donor will benefit will make a more successful drive.

Fund-Raising Techniques

There are several fund-raising techniques available to progressive churches. The most common methods are tithe donations, capital campaigns, and small pledges. Tithe donations are yearly donations of 10% of the member's income. Capital campaigns are for collecting a specific amount of money during a limited period of time. Capital campaigns require the use of volunteers and usually entail a lot of telephoning.

Small pledges are those taken from members throughout the year or for a special occasion. These donations are normally under a hundred dollars.

A large part of the prosperity of tithes, capital campaigns, and pledges are that they encourage donors to give again in the future. Once a donor has given, a church can attempt to approach them again to give a second or third time. There is the potential to make the donations yearly or even twice yearly. These three methods (tithes, campaigns, and pledges) have proven to be very useful fund-raising alternatives. They are key because most donations come from church members. Churches, however, should not limit themselves to these methods of fund-raising. Other methods of fund-raising are available such as grants (normally to fund outreach programming), memorial or honor gifts, and large donations.

Memorials, honor gifts, and large donations can be used to bring favorable results for churches. Memorial gifts are given by members through their wills or by their families in honor of them. Churches should approach potential memorial donors tactfully and with respect. Members can be told that the church accepts memorial gifts via a newsletter or other efforts. Personal contact with the potential donor should always be arranged through a visit to his or her home or a meeting in the church. Members who have been dedicated to the church will usually give, although many simply do not think of memorial gifts in their giving. It is up to the church to make them aware of this option. Churches should attain legal advice before actively soliciting memorial gifts. They entail certain legal aspects which a church may not know about. Legal advice can avoid future problems which may hamper a church's fund-raising efforts.

Honor gifts are very similar to memorial gifts except that the donor is usually alive. Honor gifts are given to recognize or acknowledge achievements or special occasions in a member's life. Churches can use the worship service as an opportunity for people to donate gifts. A gift to celebrate a wedding anniversary in commemoration of the original service performed in the church can be encouraged. Honor gifts can also be made in celebration of a member's birthday or other special occasion.

Traditionally, large donations represent only a small percentage of the total donations to a church, as many churches avoid soliciting large contributions from church and community members. But they should not. Churches should attempt to gain large donations without spending an unreasonable amount of time and money. Attaining these types of donations requires more work than other methods. Potential large donors can be found with research, and they should be approached personally rather than by mail or a newsletter. Often, repeat visits are necessary, so patience can pay off to those willing to make the extra effort. If a church acquires a large donation, there is the potential to gain a repeat contribution in the future. Ideally, a benefactor situation would be established, though this rarely happens. Realistically, most people are not able to give large ($100 or $1,000) gifts and, churches must keep this in mind in their fund-raising efforts.

Summary of Fund-Raising Methods

There are many important decisions to be made when a church begins a fund-raising campaign. A church must decide what type of fund-raising method it wants to use and how it wants to contact potential donors. Two of the easiest and widely used methods are newsletters and phone calls, which have proven successful for capital campaigns and tithe and pledge donation requests. These methods may be too informal for some fund-raising requests such as large donations. Personal interviews and direct mailing efforts can be used instead. These contacts are more expensive and time consuming, but the extra expense can be profitable for a fund-raising campaign. A church must have something to offer the potential donor to make personal interviews and direct mail succeed. They take up the potential donors' time, and they must be made to feel that they have received something in exchange for their time.

Direct mail can be an expensive undertaking. The appearance, packaging, and content of the mailing must be well planned and appealing in order to be a success. The direct mail request should give the donor options of how much to donate (highlighting the average donation amount given by others). Small touches such as including a return contribution envelope for mailing and personalizing requests (not sending stock forms) will help the mailing become a success. Thus, an updated donor list can be useful to avoid repeat and incorrect address mailings.

They key to successful fund-raising is to use the right methods at the right time.

Conclusion

A church can have a profitable fund-raising program if it does a few important things. No fund-raising effort will be successful if it has no direction. Direction comes from goal-setting, planning, and working hard. Once a church decides how much they want to raise, then they must determine the source of those funds. All of the traditional and progressive fund-raising techniques target specific audiences. The needs and economic ability of a particular group to give must be addressed to make a donation attractive to the donor. Fund-raising requests should not ask people to give beyond their means. People will not give to a church or charity if they feel that they are not benefitting by making the gift, so a church must try to fulfill its needs while fulfilling those of its donors. These are not easy things to balance, but a balance must be found if a church wants to have a productive fund-raising campaign.

There are some questions that a church can ask itself to aid in fund-raising planning. Please review the checklist section.

6

How to Secure
Corporate Sponsorship

*The wise is never grown, regardless of age,
but continues to grow.*

A recent trend in business, entertainment, and religious events is securing major corporate sponsorships and endorsements for events. There are a few basic principles which a church should know and follow to be successful in gaining a corporate sponsor for a planned event. This practice of securing corporate sponsorship is growing steadily as the corporate sector expands its realm to include new consumers and communities. Fortune 500 companies and other companies are now realizing the high marketing potential and value of church event sponsorship. In the past, many companies never considered sponsoring such events, but now they recognize how certain church-related events can fill marketing voids and increase consumer awareness. A progressive church can take advantage of this trend to help cover the costs of presenting concerts, auctions, or other events while providing a service to the corporations and better serving its community. Corporate sponsorship of church events combines marketing and community affairs, creating a direct link between the corporation and the community.

There are many benefits that can be derived by churches and sponsors from this arrangement. First, it provides an alternative way of subsidizing production costs and financing the church event. Second, it provides a mechanism for marketing the event and the corporation's product. This generates even greater revenue for both the corporation and the church. Third, a sponsorship arrangement enhances the image of the sponsor's product as well as that of the church's event through association of the product or entertainment with the wholeness of the church and community. Fourth, it creates an image of integrity for the church if the corporation advertises on a broad scale. Finally, a sponsorship arrangement can significantly reduce the church's cost of advertising the event, whether it be a concert, auction, art sale,or other event.

Sponsors are increasingly supporting local events instead of national programs. The benefits of increased revenue and business awareness from a sponsorship are more likely to become visible. Local events such as church programs, cultural programs, state fairs, athletic events, and entertainment events are generally corporate sponsored. Sponsorship of these local events gives the sponsor an opportunity to attract and target the community more so than other forms of advertisement.

Because of the cost of presenting an event, churches can share both the costs and the benefits of the project with an interested party. Corporate sponsorship provides an alternate vehicle for subsidizing these church events. A sponsorship arrangement enables the church to structure a financially conducive arrangement that is mutually beneficial for the sponsor and the church.

To take full advantage of such an arrangement, the church should control the project at the initial stage. In doing so, the church can secure whatever rights and privileges are associated with the endorsement and sponsorship potential with third parties. Many sponsor-seekers miscalculate what is the right approach for sponsorships. The church should always contact the corporation directly and avoid going through an advertising agency or other organization. Knocking on the door of a company and presenting the material improperly, however, may ruin the opportunity for sponsorship. These are the most common problems observed in presenting and securing corporate sponsorships:

1. Insufficient research on the company and its product, which results in a poorly prepared proposal
2. Ego interjection, which interferes with the presentation
3. Sponsors that have been mismatched with the event or project

Potential sponsors must be shown how they can benefit from sponsoring the church's event. If the church demonstrates how the sponsor will immediately benefit from the promotional investment, either with increased product awareness or increased profits, securing sponsorship will be easier. The best way to do this is to show some connection between the event and the product. Mismatches will not benefit the sponsor, but potential problems with matching should not deter potential sponsors and the church from trying to create new avenues for sponsorship.

It takes a substantial amount of preparation to attract a "blue chip" sponsor. A blue chip sponsor provides the most financial support. Such a sponsor can carry a large percentage, if not all, of the costs of the event. An event can have more than one sponsor, but the church must make sure that an event is not saturated with too many sponsors, which would reduce the benefits to the sponsors and the attractiveness of the deal.

A sponsor is not likely to endorse what the church presents unless there is a star or a "bankable name" associated with the project. However, there are very few stars. The church must know, therefore, how to attract a sponsor for "marginal projects," as benefits which can be gained without a star connection. To achieve this, the church's proposal must present information in a logical fashion in order for the corporation to understand the project. The proposal should be written in language familiar to the potential sponsor, and the church should know the project thoroughly and be prepared to answer questions from the sponsor of a prospective project.

The church must align the right sponsor with the event. This means both understanding the needs of the community and assessing the kinds of projects a particular corporation might be interested in. The information gained will help to create a proper presentation for the corporation. The presentation must inform the corporation about both the nature of the project and the potential rewards. If the church highlights unexplored market areas and untouched consumer demands that can be reached by sponsorship of the event, the benefits will become greater to the corporation. (See the sample model.)

The best way to prepare a presentation is by knowing the prospective sponsoring corporation. The church promoter must know

1. To whom the corporation is trying to appeal in the consumer market,
2. The past amount of money ear-marked for sponsorship, and
3. The growth direction of the corporation.

The church should also know how the corporation works, that is, how decisions are made, and who makes them. Knowing the company will help the church demonstrate the benefits of being associated with the event, and this knowledge will enable the church to better serve the corporation. The sponsorship arrangement must be cost-effective so the sponsor will be motivated, if necessary, to divert the dollars that may have been considered for allocation to other projects.

Churches should also be aware of the tax implications of corporate sponsorship. In the past, the Internal Revenue Service declared that corporate sponsorship funds were taxable as advertisement expenditures versus tax-exempt charitable donations. The church should consult an attorney to ascertain the applicable current tax laws and avoid any tax problems. This consultation should be done before the corporation is approached.

Conclusion

Corporate sponsorship of church events is a growing and highly productive form of defraying the costs of producing an event. The costs of presenting major church events are rising and can be overwhelming for a church to absorb independently. Corporate sponsorship can provide the funds necessary for an event while providing a service to the corporation and the community.

There are certain steps which a church must take in preparing to approach a potential sponsor. A crucial factor is researching the corporation and knowing as much as possible about it. Knowing how the corporation targets its audience, its needs, and how it spends its money will help the church prepare a professional and effective presentation. The corporation must be shown the potential benefits, such as profits and increased consumer awareness, to help the event appear more attractive to the sponsor. Once this is accomplished, churches can present events more effectively at less cost. Providing these events will help the community, while more time can be spent presenting a variety of other services.

7

Ancillary Functions of a Progressive Church

Miracles can happen when
we recognize that we can do for ourselves.

CHURCHES AND COMMUNITY DEVELOPMENT CORPORATIONS

As churches have become more progressive in their efforts to meet the needs of both the members of their church and the surrounding area, the creation of Community Development Corporations (CDCs) have become the vehicle of choice to effectuate a positive outward ministry to create housing, economic development, and job opportunities. CDCs are legal corporations created under state law to promote neighborhood development. They are formed no differently than regular corporations, with the exception that they are generally formed under a nonprofit corporation act, and are generally formed as 501(c)(3) tax-exempt organizations.

CDCs have become the vehicle of choice for most church organizations to promote three goals: (1) economic development, (2) housing, and (3) job training. This has occurred as a result of legislation enacted by Congress that has encouraged the use of CDCs to receive federal grants and loans for rehabilitation projects in the areas mentioned above. In addition, private philanthropic organizations are encouraging organizations that wish to receive funding for CDC's with their own contributions.

What Is a CDC Composed of?

The composition of a CDC is really no different from any other organization. Typically, they have a Board of Directors that establishes the broad policy under which the organization will operate. In selecting the members of your Board of Directors, the church wants to be selective in choosing persons who represent a broad section of the church community and who will actively participate in the direction of the organization. Initially, the church may select five directors during the formative stages of its development while leaving itself the latitude to appoint additional directors when new responsibilities arise.

Depending on the financial strength of the organization, your church CDC may have an Executive Director who is responsible for carrying out the day-to-day responsibilities of the organization. Initially, the Executive Director's primary responsibility may be to assist in stabilizing funding for the organization and implementing the policy directives of the Board. The Executive Director's responsibilities will expand as funding increases.

Staff personnel are added as the CDC grows. In some instances, CDCs initially start off with a large Board of Directors that delegates the responsibilities for implementing Board policy and fundraising until such time as an Executive Director is hired to further stabilize the funding of the organization and additional staff recruited.

The traditional model of a CDC varies depending on the needs of the church. As noted above, some CDCs stress three areas of involvement: (1) economic development through the creation of equity funds to promote business development, (2) neighborhood revitalization through the implementation of rehabilitation programs for housing in areas around the church, and (3) job training.

Neighborhood Revitalization

Neighborhood revitalization through the implementation of housing rehabilitation programs often serves as the cornerstone for church community development corporations. Churches in urban areas, in particular, have taken advantage of this tool to promote neighborhood stabilization around their boundaries. Oftentimes the church CDC will start out rehabilitating a dilapidated structure close to its boundaries. Most of the materials and supplies for the rehabilitation of the home may be donated, with the church members donating sweat equity to make repairs. Once completed, the home is then rented out, or sold to raise money for funding other housing developments.

As the CDC becomes more adept at rehabilitation, they often move into new multi-family construction. Because the rent structure of some of these facilities may not necessarily support the debt service on mortgage payments on the property, the use of tax credits authorized under the Internal Revenue Code is often an integral part of the financial package needed to make a project a reality. Dependent upon the Board's sophistication of the CDC, some CDCs have simply donated the land toward the project in an effort to take a percentage of the overall development.

Job Training

Housing rehabilitation naturally creates the job-training component of the CDC through sweat equity rehabilitation work. The primary job-training opportunities arise in those areas where minorities have historically not been represented in the skilled trades such as rough carpentry, painting, drywalling, and masonry. Church CDCs can often team up with a skills training program in existence with a local school district's adult education program which offers training in the skilled trade areas mentioned above or work with a local union hall which will provide technical assistance to the CDC.

A number of persons who have provided sweat equity towards rehabilitation projects have gone on to form companies which specialize in rehabilitation. When seeking to identify business opportunities for your church CDC members, you should keep this in mind. Once the church members of a CDC have become proficient in doing a particular job, many churches have created private corporations, owned by the church, to go out and bid on other church CDC work or for private businesses. This additional source of income can be helpful in stabilizing church finances and the community.

Venture Capital

Church CDCs serve as a source of venture capital, funding which provides a source of equity for businesses which are not financially strong enough to grow. Venture capital funding requires a great deal of sophistication and money in the hands of the CDC. The sophistication comes in having Board members or an Executive Director who has the financial strength of a particular business, who can accurately assess the business position of the entity, and who makes strong recommendations as to how the CDC will benefit by making a proposed investment in the organization.

The ability of the CDC to risk capital is tied totally to the size of the CDC's capital base, its ability to accurately gage the risks it is willing to undertake, and the amount of money it can afford to lose. While there are a number of governmental programs to assist in the formation of church CDC venture capital funds, there are a limited number of dollars to support such ventures.

Benefits to the Church in Forming a CDC

How does a church benefit from forming a CDC? First, the church benefits by expanding its outreach efforts to assist persons outside the walls of its sanctuary. CDCs by their very nature involve changing the environment of people through positive outreach efforts. These outreach efforts will have a profound influence when it, for example, provides safe and sanitary housing for a family that previously lived in substandard housing.

It can become financially beneficial for a church that is looking for alternative ways to raise money. As discussed in this section, the business spin-off possibilities can create substantial financial security to those church CDCs who are astute enough to take advantage of them.

Overview of Forming a
Nonprofit Community Development Corporation

1. The church must have its Board of Directors (Deacons and Trustees) authorize the formation of a nonprofit Community Development Corporation.
2. Drafts of Articles of Incorporation and Bylaws should be prepared and reviewed by an attorney.
3. The Articles of Incorporation and Bylaws must be filed with the Corporations & Securities Bureau (CSB) of the Department of Commerce. There is a small filing fee.
4. Once the Articles of Incorporation and Bylaws have been reviewed and accepted, a number will be assigned by the CSB for the non-

profit corporation. This is a separate number for the CDC, and its books and records should be kept separate from the Church's.

5. A separate Board of Directors should be established for the CDC and corporate officers selected. This Board should be comprised of those persons within the church who have experience in the following areas: law, accounting, construction, job training, grant applications, or business development. The pastor should stress that persons on the Board should be committed to providing service to the CDC, and that back-up assistance will be available through the First Independence Community Development Bank (FICDB) Advisory Board of Detroit, Michigan.

6. Once the corporate number has been assigned to the nonprofit development corporation, an application for 501(c)(3) tax-exempt status should be filed with the Internal Revenue Service. This will allow donations made to the CDC to be deductible for contributors to the CDC.

7. The IRS will review the application for nonprofit status and issue a determination letter that the corporation is exempt from taxation and authorized to accept donations.

8. Once the IRS designation is in place, the CDC should move into action by determining its first project. Evaluation of your first project should take into account the Board of Directors' consultation with the FICDB.

CHURCH MODEL (CDC)

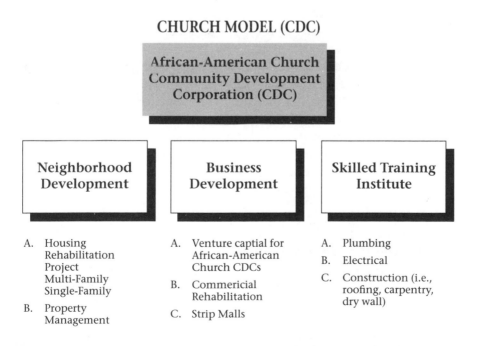

African-American Church Community Development Corporation (CDC)

Neighborhood Development

Business Development

Skilled Training Institute

A. Housing Rehabilitation Project
   Multi-Family
   Single-Family

B. Property Management

A. Venture captial for African-American Church CDCs

B. Commericial Rehabilitation

C. Strip Malls

A. Plumbing

B. Electrical

C. Construction (i.e., roofing, carpentry, dry wall)

BANK MODEL

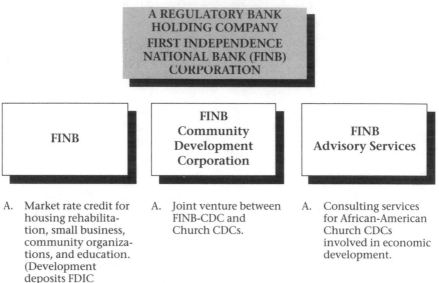

A REGULATORY BANK HOLDING COMPANY FIRST INDEPENDENCE NATIONAL BANK (FINB) CORPORATION

FINB	**FINB Community Development Corporation**	**FINB Advisory Services**
A. Market rate credit for housing rehabilitation, small business, community organizations, and education. (Development deposits FDIC insured)	A. Joint venture between FINB-CDC and Church CDCs.	A. Consulting services for African-American Church CDCs involved in economic development.

Joint Ventures: An Idea Whose Time Has Come

Should churches consider entering into joint ventures? The decision requires an awareness of both the advantages and disadvantages involved.

First, the advantages:

1. Give the opportunity to present a broad cross section of community facilities and participation.
2. Provide cost effective advice and support during the early start-up period when expertise and resources are in short supply.
3. Insure that the goals of the CDC/Joint Venture are targeted to the community's needs and resources.
4. Provide realistic strategies for development that may be crucial to access new resources, both private and public.
5. Provide a crucial network of economic resources in order to provide expanded economies of scale.

Now the disadvantages:

1. Time commitments of volunteers may be limited, thereby limiting the scope of their participation.
2. Relations between the various joint venture partners can slow the decision-making process.
3. Competing or inconsistent goals may force uneventful working relationships.

THE CHURCH AND SENIOR CITIZEN HOUSING

The number of citizens over age 65 is growing daily. With the increase in the number of senior citizens, the need for more adequate housing becomes clear. This growing segment of our population has specific needs which differ from the rest of the population. Senior citizens need special health care and social activities to combat social isolation. Proper housing can provide all these things and bring new life to a community. For churches interested in such ventures there is federal funding available, as well as tax-exempt financing in some states.

Churches must keep in mind that all senior citizen housing is not alike. There are numerous types of housing designs possible to suit the various needs of seniors. With each type of design there are benefits and problems. The cost difference to construct the various forms of senior citizen housing must be considered. When deciding to establish senior citizen housing many things must be considered. A few basic things must be determines:

1. Location
2. Size
3. Structural style (high-rise or scattered)
4. Types of services that will be offered (housekeeping, health care, food service, etc.)

Location is key to a senior citizen housing project. Senior citizens living on their own are most often isolated from the rest of the community. Senior citizen housing projects must do what it can to prevent this. A successful housing project should be located so as to take advantage of the public transportation system and nearby commercial businesses. A strategically located housing project should offer more to its residents. Many federal grants and financing programs also demand that senior citizen housing projects be located within a close vicinity of commercial businesses such as grocery stores and shopping centers. The purpose of the housing project is to make life easier and less stressful for senior citizens. A convenient location will easily satisfy these necessities. Unfortunately, land near commercial businesses may be more expensive to purchase than land located elsewhere.

Once a church has determined where it wants to build the housing project, several other decisions need to be made. The size and style of the project must be determined. The larger the project the more expensive it will be to build and maintain. A large project, however, can be successful if it does not pass on too much of the extra costs to its residents.

Two of the most popular styles of senior citizen housing are the high-rise and scattered.

A high-rise style project requires less land to build and many believe that it is easier to build in urban areas. Some, however, argue that the high-rise style isolates seniors from the rest of the community because little interaction is possible. An alternative style is scattered or separate buildings. These types of housing units form their own community or can be integrated into an existing community. This gives the seniors some autonomy while preserving a community atmosphere. This style requires more land for construction than the high-rise form. Both styles, however, must fulfill the particular zoning standards of their area and can be adapted to fit the needs of its senior residents. A church must remember that senior citizens require more than just shelter to satisfy their special needs.

Senior citizen housing projects should provide services to make the seniors lives more comfortable. On-site services have been the most successful and are used more often by seniors. One type of housing is a retirement community. A retirement community usually does not offer health care facilities for its residents, but it allows them to own their own home or condominium within the community. Assisted living facilities are for those senior citizens who require 24-hour care. Their meals are prepared for them, and a fully staffed medical team is usually in residence. These two forms of housing are great for senior citizens who have a comfortable amount of money. These types of housing projects require significant funds to maintain and build. Churches must consider the economic aspects of senior citizen housing when deciding what type to build.

One of the easiest, most popular, and least expensive forms of housing is congregate housing. It offers services geared toward the independent senior who needs some medical help and encouragement to socialize. Congregate housing offers a food service which is served in a community eating area much like a college dormitory. Housekeeping services and some health care are generally offered. These services can be offered as optional at a separate charge from the resident's rent, or they can be included in the rent charge. The more services a housing project offers, the more time it leaves its residents to socialize and relax and enjoy their later years in life.

The cost of building and maintaining senior citizen housing must be considered. Some funding for constructing senior citizen housing can be gained from the federal government; specifically the Department of Housing and Urban Development (HUD). HUD gives funds most often for congregate housing projects which fulfill its criteria on size and services, etc. There are also other federal grants available to churches under the heading of community development funds. The government sets aside these funds because it recognizes the need for adequate senior citizen housing. A few states, such as Georgia, offer tax-exempt financing for nonprofit organizations to build and maintain senior citizen housing. The church should contact their local government (both city and state) and the federal government to find out the availability of funding.

Funding which is available is generally reserved for nonprofit organizations only. Though churches are often declared nonprofit, they should not take on the endeavor of building senior citizen housing. Churches should create a separate nonprofit, tax-exempt organization to handle the housing project. This should be done to prevent a conflict with the church's primary function. If the IRS determines that the housing project creates such a conflict, then the church could lose its tax-exempt status and become liable for back taxes. Therefore, to avoid tax problems, a church should establish a separate nonprofit, tax-exempt organization. Any church which is confused or unclear as to how to do this should consult an attorney on how to properly establish such a separate organization.

Please also review the checklist on page 130 for an overview of steps the church should follow to strategically set up a senior citizen housing project.

Conclusion

The elderly population of this country is growing, and with this growth comes the need for more senior citizen housing. Churches have an opportunity to provide such a service to aid their older congregation members and community residents. Though some churches may not realize it, they have an advantage over many commercial developers of senior citizen housing. The church already has a body of potential tenants/residents within its congregation. It does not have to worry about whether there will be people to fill their housing project. The type of housing that the church decides to build hinges upon the amount of money it wants to spend and charge its residents. The land, building, and services that can be offered vary in price and cost.

The location and amount of services offered depends greatly upon the needs of the senior residents. A senior citizen housing project which costs too much for its residents to afford will ultimately fail. A church which keeps abreast of the needs of the community and its financial condition will be better able to determine appropriate costs and become successful. A church should consider establishing a separate nonprofit organization to handle the creation of senior citizen housing.

DAY-CARE CENTERS

Providing a day-care service is one of the best ways in which a church can service its congregation and community. In today's society, both parents are usually full-time workers, leaving the care of their children to others. A church can implement a day-care center for the children of its community while nurturing the child's development. More is involved in providing day-care centers than merely caring and "looking after" the children. Children have very specific educational, emotional, and physical needs. Satisfying these needs can be accomplished with proper planning and care.

Fulfilling State Requirements

Most day-care centers are licensed or regulated by the state. Churches should inquire of the State Department of Social Services about the specific requirements in their states. Minimum health, safety, staff training, and child-adult ratio characteristics are usually all a state requires. A few states, however, only ask that a day-care center register with its Department of Social Services. Legal advice from an attorney should be attained to ensure that a church learns and fulfills all of its particular state requirements. Failure to comply with regulations can prevent a day-care center from opening or forcing an existing day-care center to close.

States usually dictate what should be the minimum educational requirements of staff members. This is done, theoretically, to protect the children from incompetent care. A properly trained staff can better service children and help them develop healthfully. Churches should employ trained professionals, as well as seek the aid of both young and older volunteers. Churches must be very selective as to who they allow to work with the children. In recent years, charges of sexual and physical abuse of children in day-care centers have risen substantially. A good staff can avoid these potentially disastrous problems.

Logistics of a Day-Care Center

Once a church has researched the basic requirements of a day-care center, the logistics of planning can begin. The church must decide who (what age group of children) they want to service within its center. There are several major age groups of day-care children: infants, toddlers, pre-school, and school-aged. Each of these groups of children have particular needs and demands. Infants and toddlers, for instance, require constant attention and care. States strongly regulate this level of child care because of the high potential of harm and vulnerability of the children. A high ratio of adults per child is also necessary to provide adequate care for children this age, which means that more jobs are available.

Pre-school and school-aged children require less care but more educational attention. Preschoolers exert some independence and show an extreme curiosity for life. Day-care centers need to nurture this curiosity and help prepare the children for future learning and social experiences. Providing educational activities throughout the day will meet this need.

School-aged children require much less supervision. Before- or after-school programs may be scheduled. Their education will consume most of their day, so a center must be supportive of them in other ways. An after-school tutorial program is one of the best ways to help school aged children. A church's day-care center can service more than one of these age groups if their activities are complementary.

Planning a Day-Care Center

Regardless of which age group a church favors, planning is essential in the development of a successful day-care center. Not only is the age group of the children important, but also the number of children the church plans to serve. Estimated enrollment will determine how large a center will have to be and what programs can feasibly be offered. Most day-care centers offer physical and educational activities such as reading and developmental skill activities and field trips. Some also offer meal services, transportation (pick up or drop off), and tutorial programs. The ease of coordinating these programs will be determined by the training and effectiveness of the staff.

Programs, salaries, equipment, and supplies cost money. These costs can be covered by contributions, state or federal funding, or fees charged to parents. The average cost of day-care (for a parent) per child ranges from $10 a week to over $200 a week. A church must be aware of how much its community is able to pay before passing on high costs to the parents. If parents cannot afford to send their children to the center, then the center will fail.

At one time federal and state funding for developing day-care centers were abundant, but that time has passed. There are still some available funding programs, and a church must research to find them. The programs usually require that the day-care center satisfy particular requirements such as providing meal services to low income children.

Contributions from the church and its members can be used to alleviate some of the economic pressure of running a day-care center. As with other outreach programs, churches should establish a separate nonprofit organization to oversee the center. This will avoid potential tax problems in the future.

Conclusion

It is possible for a church to successfully operate a day-care center with proper planning. Deciding who will work in the center and the target age-group of children will produce a solid foundation for other work. In determining these factors, churches must remain aware of the needs of not only themselves, but particularly the children. Children are exceptional human beings, and they need understanding, guidance, and educational and social experiences. A church can provide all of these. The design of the day-care center should be planned with economics in mind. The cost to parents must be reasonable. Outside funding can be sought to reduce the financial burden on the parents and the church. Providing a day-care center can bring a community closer to a church and provide a safe and nurturing environment for children.

DRUG ABUSE TREATMENT/OUTREACH PROGRAMS

There is a growing need for drug treatment and counseling facilities in cities and towns throughout the country. Drugs are destroying families, individuals, and communities. Many churches can be tremendously helpful and instrumental in combatting the problem. Churches have the time, space, and means to provide treatment and counseling services to alleviate some of the damages that drug abuse cause. There are several different approaches to providing drug treatment and counseling programs. The goals, theories, and the amount of resources that a church has will decide which particular approach a church uses. Equally important in determining which approach to use are the needs of the abuser and victims in the general community. Programs that do not satisfy these needs will not be successful.

A church must determine a few things before it embarks upon a drug treatment or counseling program. The church should determine which segment of the drug-using population it wants to help. Drug use affects people of all ages—children, teens, and adults, including pregnant women. There are certain risks associated with helping each of these groups. Also important is the particular drug addiction that the program will address. Alcohol and narcotics are both drugs which have a tremendous affect on people. They, however, require different treatments and counseling techniques. A church should be aware of this when developing its programs.

The church must look to its own community and congregation to find out where it can be most effective. It is best to tailor the program to the particular problem that is most prevalent in the church's community. This will help the church aid its community and fulfill its needs.

Drug Treatment Programs

Though many people interchange the terms "drug treatment"and "drug counseling," they are two very different things. Drug treatment is usually a medically supervised or influenced program which helps the addict reduce and end drug use. Oftentimes, legal prescription drugs are prescribed to alleviate the harshness of withdrawal which most addicts experience while quitting drug use. These programs can be in-house, where the patient lives for a specified time or until they are drug free. The program can also be out-patient where the patient goes home after treatment and is less supervised. The term "patient" is used because one of the basic theories of this type of facility is that drug addiction is a disease and that there is a cure (the proper amount of medication and lifestyle change).

A church that wishes to establish a drug treatment facility must consider several things. Because most drug treatment centers prescribe drugs to counter the effects of the illegal drug use, the staff must be professionally trained. A doctor and several nurses will be required to operate such a facility effectively. It is best that the entire treatment staff have some medical training. A staff such as this can be expensive to maintain, but there are ways to reduce the financial strain.

The church should try to provide its program in conjunction with a local hospital or clinic. Many hospitals and clinics are more than willing to lend their staff members (for a small fee) to community-based programs. Hospitals do not have enough room in their buildings to serve the amount of patients, so the church will help to reduce the hospital's strain. Once the particular program and its logistics are established, a church representative can approach the hospital with a proposal. The church can collect funds from members, patients, federal or state aid, insurance coverage, and other organizations to provide this service.

Drug Counseling Programs

Drug treatment programs are vastly different from drug counseling programs. Drug counseling programs usually do not prescribe drugs or offer extensive medical help. Instead, a drug counseling center does exactly that—counsel. Most drug addicts refuse to admit that they are addicted; therefore, they do not seek treatment. Drug counseling tries to help the addicts realize that they have a drug problem and to do something about the addiction. The counseling is both educational and directional. A good program will offer options for the addict, such as how to become involved in the program and how to end the addiction.

Drug addiction in this type of program is treated more from a psychological point of view rather than a "disease" perspective. Addicts are often shown why they use drugs. A basic theory is that something is missing from the addict's life and the drugs fill this void or at least make them forget that the void exists. Counseling offers the addict more positive alternatives as to how to fill this void and avoid drug use. One of the most famous drug counseling programs is Alcoholics Anonymous, where the addict goes though various stages to eventually terminate the drug use.

A drug counseling program presents different obstacles to a church. This type of program is less expensive than drug treatment programs, but it has other problems. At first glance it would seem as if anyone can do drug counseling, but this is not the case. Improper treatment can hurt an addict more than help them. Staff members should be trained in counseling and some psychology. A pastor should already have some of these skills. Surprisingly, ex-addicts who have gone through the process are some of the best staff members. They relate to the addicts in the program and can offer first hand advice. A drug counseling program should never try to treat addicts with medicine, but it can refer them to a treatment center whenever needed.

Conclusion

Drugs have a profound effect on society today. The number of addicts, drug-addicted babies, and people dying of AIDS (from sharing needles) is growing everyday. Though a solution to the dilemma may seem far off, churches can help in solving the problem. Church-based drug treatment and counseling programs can be used to help those who cannot get help elsewhere. The church should determine its needs and abilities. Proper planning and organization can make the establishing of either program possible. Once this has been done, then it can begin creating a program to satisfy the needs of its community.

Drug counseling and treatment programs can be combined to better service the addict. The costs and problems of embarking on such an endeavor must be considered and addressed. The church should consult with an attorney on the legal ramifications to find out if any state licensing is required and to determine if the program will affect the church's tax-exempt status. Even with these factors in mind, the progressive church must remember that the rewards of having such a program are great.

It is always prudent to set up the church ancillary programs as follows. The church must decide whether to be a separate entity or a foundation with a separate entity to protect the tax-exempt status of the church in the event of legal problems such as state or tax auditing consequences from third parties.

FOOD CO-OPERATIVES

Any organization, church group, or religious organization with the desire and the will to do so can create a food co-op that suits their needs if they have the necessary information. The purpose of this chapter is to provide information in such a way that a church or church affiliated group can form and operate a food co-op for the benefit of its congregation and the surrounding communities as well as positively contributing to the control and destiny of the community.

There is no single definition of a food co-operative which encompasses all food co-ops simply because the function and purposes of each vary to serve the diverse needs of its members. However in most basic terms, a food co-op is defined as "a group of people who have gotten together to cope with high food prices," propelled by skyrocketing food costs, improper food handling, supermarket scandals, and dissatisfied consumers.

Because of the public outcry, food co-ops have emerged as a viable solution to supermarket woes. Although food co-ops have traditionally developed as an outgrowth of dissatisfied neighbors or communities, their use has currently expanded into a highly effective tool utilized by community organizations, such as churches, as a low-cost food source for the underprivileged and inner-city residents. In Philadelphia, the Archdiocese's Neighborhood Nutrition Program directs food co-operatives in order to obtain reasonable food prices for inner city communities. While food co-ops are not the answer in all situations, it is certainly an option worthy of consideration by any progressive church.

Forming a Co-Operative

Once a church makes the decision as to how to set up and how it is to be organized, it must then consider several important factors. These include the form of the organization, whether to incorporate as a non-stock or stock co-op, and what to include in the bylaws.

Deciding Whether to Incorporate

The directors of a food co-op should give serious consideration to incorporating where a number of members are involved, and the accumulation of capital is required before or after operations. Other factors to be considered when incorporating include whether the membership will change from time to time or remain the same, whether the lifetime of the operation is for a fixed period or is intended to continue indefinitely, and whether it should be incorporated as a non-stock membership corporation or as a membership corporation with capital stock.

A non-stock membership co-op is not, conceptually, significantly different from any other kind of non-stock membership corporation. Non-stock membership co-ops eliminate much of the paper work and bookkeeping associated with the issuance and transfer of stock certificates without significant loss in financial flexibility. In addition, incorporating as a non-stock membership can minimize, but not altogether eliminate, the possibility of the co-op being classified as a security, which can translate into mounds of needless legal red tape in the form of federal and state securities regulation. Adherence to these securities regulations in turn can delay or prevent the acceptance of new members.

Stock co-ops also have advantages and disadvantages. A stock co-op is composed of members and shareholders, with only members having the right to vote. If more than one class of capital stock exists, the articles of incorporation should indicate which class of stock will identify the voting members. Stock co-ops can also avoid regulation since all such co-ops are not always considered to be securities by courts. Additionally, many states have statutes which hold a certain dollar amount of membership shares exempt from securities regulation. Accordingly, in communities where multiple stock co-ops are already in existence, the organization should follow the trend.

ANCILLARY FUNCTIONS OF A PROGRESSIVE CHURCH

The only additional regulations which a food co-op may be subject to may arise if the co-op needs to qualify for state tax-exemption, or if the group plans to apply for authorization to accept food stamps.

Many states have a sales tax on food. If the food co-op is located in such a state, then it will be necessary to obtain a sales tax-exemption or certificate. Since the process for securing exempt status varies from state to state, church representatives should contact the local branch of the state sales tax office or the state department of public welfare for information on the subject.

Authorization to accept food stamps is granted by the local office of the United States Department of Agriculture Food Stamp office. In order to receive authorization, the group generally must be incorporated as a nonprofit organization. The co-op must obtain a *federal* tax-exempt certificate which can then be used to obtain a *state* nonprofit recognition certificate. In some states, no further action is required. However, in other states, the state certificate will be used to obtain a certificate from the *city* tax office. Then three copies of the co-op's bylaws, as well as information on when and where the food is distributed, should be filed with the city health inspector's office or the city health department.

Upon presentation of the required certificates from the federal, state, city and health agencies, the USDA Food Stamp office will issue a license or authorization card, and special bank deposit slips for use in depositing the food stamps in the bank. The card will permit the group to use food stamps to purchase the food from a store.

However, aside from satisfying the legal requirements necessary for the formation of a food co-op, there remain some practical considerations which are equally critical.

First, the members must commit to the goal of building a food co-op. Next the group should conduct research of the types of food that the group would like to buy (e.g., health foods, meats, fish), and then one must investigate sources (e.g., wholesale, retail) for such foods.

It is important to use an organized method for selecting the foods to buy which will meet the different needs of its members. Where the target membership is very expansive as in a church congregation, it is recommended that the co-op sticks to basic foods from each of the food groups rather than relying on individual preferences of its members. The church may develop its own system designed to meet the needs of its members regardless of which system is used to maximize efficiency. The co-op should eliminate items that receive this minimum support, as well as those items that are sold close to wholesale prices at other grocery stores.

After determining the goods to be purchased, finding the source for the foods that the co-op desires to purchase is next on the church's agenda. There are several popular sources. Wholesale food outlets are easiest to locate in urban areas and are the most common starting points. Wholesale distributors may be located in the yellow pages under Food Products and Suppliers listings. The directors of the food co-op may also learn of additional food sources by speaking with cooks, nutritionists or members of institutional kitchen staffs. Church representatives should also attempt to contact area farmers directly. This can be done by contacting the local or regional branch of the Department of Agriculture of Future Farmers of America.

After discovering a food source, the members of the food co-op should obtain pricing information. The price of the food is generally determined by the size of the order and the bulk quantity that the foods are available for purchase. In researching the available foods and their respective costs, the members of the co-op should obtain the following information from distributors:

1. The distributor's business hours
2. Whether accepted payment should be cash only or cash and checks
3. Whether they have a delivery service
4. When payment is due
5. What the refund policy is
6. How to acquire current information on products available and price changes

Finally, the members of the food co-op must determine the type of equipment needed to effectively operate the co-op and designate a place where the goods will be stored and distributed. Some of the basic items needed for operating a co-op include drivers (to sources of supply), vehicles for transportation, and people to load and unload the vehicle. Additional essentials may include volunteers, weight scales, storage facilities to aid in the preservation of products; smaller items such as brooms, dustpans, mops, pencils, marking pens, tape, scissors, cheese-cutting knife, used egg cartons, and paper bags are also necessary items.

Every food co-op must have a distribution center from which to dispense its goods. There are 6 features that a co-op should consider when selecting a site. The site should

1. Be large enough to house large crates, boxes, and baskets which will be moved from place to place
2. Be sheltered from the elements

3. Be well-lit to allow for the reading of small numbers and mimeo-graphed sheets
4. Have an easily cleaned floor
5. Be readily accessible to water
6. Be close to both the wholesaler and the members

After the church leaders have completed these preliminary considerations the church will be ready to establish a system for distributing the goods.

Managing the Food Co-Operative

Once the initial ground work has been laid for the formation of the co-op, the church representatives should make decisions regarding designation of an official mailing address for the group, determination of the length of time that should be allowed to elapse between purchases, the frequency of membership meetings, and a system for collection of money. An official mailing address should be designated to receive catalogues, price lists, bank statements, Department of Agriculture market news publications, and other materials. Similarly, if food is to be delivered, a site must also be designated.

The length of time between purchases should be set as well as general purchases. As a rule, purchases are to be made in weekly, bi-weekly, or monthly intervals based upon the demand and turnover of the co-op and its members.

Membership meetings should be conducted with appropriate frequency to discuss co-op business. A decision should be made by members whether meetings will be held on a regular weekly or monthly basis or as the need may arise.

Final considerations which often generate the most concern are staffing and the collection of money. Finances can generally be divided into two main categories: money *collected* from members, and money *paid* to food sources.

Money is collected from members generally in two ways: membership fees and operational expenses. Most food co-ops adopt the policy of collecting a one-time-only membership from its participants. The fee generally ranges from 50 cents to $20 per person. Records should be kept to reflect who has made such payments. Some food co-ops also collect money for initial start up expenses and extra expenses that arise periodically, so the group must additionally develop a system for collecting such monies. A complete system for shopping, packing food, and allocating the work (whether volunteer or paid) must be established.

Conclusion

The potential good to be served by the formation of a food co-op is only limited by the willingness of its members or the church body to commit to organization and execution of its operation. In the long run, it is a valuable and worthwhile investment to its members which deserves the consideration of any progressive church.[*]

FINANCIAL INVESTMENT FOR CHURCHES

Many black churches today have to face rapid change in developing and preserving its resources to meet growing demands.

In examining church portfolios, I find that many churches put hundreds of thousands of dollars in a passbook savings account. First of all, they should know that under the Insurance Banking Act, only $500,000.00 can be protected due to banking regulations (and this amount could change in the future).

The concepts put forth here are based on the lack of essential investment understanding in directing the resources of a church, particularly a black church. Therefore, the church should upgrade its thinking and seek professional help to stabilize itself and ensure the security of its capital.

The church can no longer deposit its money in just one place and relax and wait confidently for it to grow. There are no totally safe and sure investments anymore. Banks have been foreclosed upon in the 1980s and the 1990s. The church should diversify its portfolio in order to protect its resources. Committees should be appointed to select a broker or financial consultant to help maintain this portfolio. This requires a greater amount of attention than in the past. To make the church investment choice even more difficult, a major shift in inflation, headed into single-digit territory, weakens the prospect of all those inflation havens of the past decade.

Other financial goals should be established for economic empowerment. Many churches do not have this empowerment as a goal and lack the direction to utilize their resources to the highest level to take care of its members and develop the community. Money has merely been left in idle accounts. Many churches use these resources to build larger churches but implement no other type of development or stabilizing programs. Therefore, a financial strategy should be established in terms of economic empowerment.

How to Start

Before the church invests in anything that has the slightest risk, make sure that its portfolio is diversified in order to preserve its resources. The trustees should become fully educated in this area before any investing or diversifying takes place. Securing the right consultant and advisor will eliminate a great deal of stress and anxiety, as well as insure the protection of the money. It is deemed that most churches are conservative and should invest in safe and steady returns of income. Since the church is not a taxable entity in preserving its money, it could take one of the more steady returns of investment income, as well as the highest, from that point of view.

Many churches that have not invested before are wondering how to start and how to diversify their portfolio. If the church is in that position, then it needs an investment strategy. Start by analyzing the present and future financial needs of the church. Define the financial goals and how the church intends to reach them. If your goal is to set up a credit union or housing project, then you should determine how much money will be needed to achieve the objective.

One of the ways to eliminate a great deal of time is to put a percentage aside toward a mutual fund. Not only would this save a great deal of time, but it would also minimize certain risks. However, the proper mutual fund must be selected in order to do so.

My recommendation is that the church should *not* invest in stocks unless they are very conservative, blue-chip stocks such as Walt Disney or certain automotive companies. The stocks in total should not be a major portion of the church portfolio. Stock options depend on the status of certain industries at the particular time. Therefore, as previously indicated, a broker or consultant should be employed.

The church should develop a strategy to endure various seasons and cycles regardless of economic trends or downfalls which the church has no control over or may not be able to predict.

It cannot be overlooked that almost all investments have some risk, but it should not stop the church from investing because even banks have risks. Sometimes the most unwise strategy is to do nothing. Churches must analyze their own situations to decide which risks they are willing to take based upon their resources, and which risks they want most to avoid.

Above all, the trustees of the church will want to protect the principal. That is, to make sure that the church does not wind up with less cash than it started out with. Also, the members and trustees will need to protect the church against interest rate fluctuation.

Getting Professional Investment Advisors

The process of choosing investment advisors has greatly changed over the past several years due to the growth in industry. Fortunately, high-grade help is more widely available now more than ever before. One of the choices is that the trustees may choose to work with the party that manages the mutual funds and offers the advantage of greater diversification than you can get with an independent advisor; management fees are usually one-third as high.

Firms are flexible as well. Firms that are willing to handle small amounts of capital typically require a minimum investment of only $1,000. They allow the church to shift its investment strategy as market conditions change. You can switch the money from one fund to another for a nominal cost. Most mutual funds do not involve a great deal of personal contact with the Board of Trustees. So an ill-informed Board of Trustees might cash in at just the wrong time. By contrast, if the church or investors have a personal investment advisor, the professional help may save them or have them wait out a bad investment time period.

An investment advisor is different from a financial planner. The former recommends specific investments and tells you when to buy and sell. The latter surveys the church's whole financial picture and suggests ways to apportion its assets and channel them into savings or annuities, as well as other possible investments.

The Board of Trustees should be diligent to develop and take out a line of credit as the plans go forward. This will help stabilize them in their mission of developing themselves and becoming economically independent.

The church cannot overlook seeking and consulting professional help in balancing its portfolios. There are many options to choose from to preserve capital in which the church does not have to invest all its resources. Then, when building an extension or securing new church property, provided that its portfolio has been properly maintained, it may be used as collateral rather than having members overextend themselves to help to build another dream.

It is imperative that the church take greater note in handling its resources in order to revitalize its mission to be a part of the economic development and to be truly progressive in the twenty-first century.

CREDIT UNION FORMATION

Why Form a Credit Union?

In considering today's economic times, the church community may occasionally have difficulties in securing money for emergency purposes, whether it be for personal or educational needs. An alternative for addressing this need is to establish a credit union as part of the church organizational structure. Some churches do provide such services. Churches that provide this service may need to upgrade diversity of capital requirements in order to yield the best financial return for its members. On the other hand, those churches that do not provide such services may wish to form a credit union. The following considerations may influence your decision: A well-run credit union can be profitable and create additional revenue for the church, or it may provide a source of funds where members may be excluded from securing access to funds from other institutions, or it may serve emergency purposes or educational needs.

How to Form a Credit Union

For a church or organization to form a credit union, there must be a common bond based upon the following:

1. Occupation
2. Association
3. Defined neighborhood
4. Geographical proximity of personal acquaintances, community interest, activities, and objectives

For example, the bond may be a common employer, a church, or a lodge. Experience has proven there must be a potential for at least 500 to 1,000 primary members in order to achieve reasonable success in providing this type of service.

To organize a credit union, one should contact the state regulatory agency of that particular state. General procedures and requirements are as follows:

1. The applicant shall file an application on forms furnished by the commissioner. The application shall state:

    a. The name and location of the proposed credit union.
    b. The names and addresses of the organizers and the number of shares subscribed by each. There is a minimum number of organizers per state; some states may require seven (7) organizers.
    c. The par value of the shares of the credit union which shall not exceed $_____ each.
    d. Such other information as the state may require

2. The application shall be forwarded to the agency, together with the filing fee, which shall be paid to the state agency to the credit of the general fund.

3. Within _____ days after receipt of an application, the regulatory agency shall determine whether or not the organization of the proposed credit union would benefit its members; that a firm commitment to insure share and deposit accounts has been issued under the provisions of Title II of the National Credit Union Act up to the maximum provided by that act; and that it will be consistent with the purposes of this act. The approval for permission to organize a credit union is discretionary with the state agency.

4. The agency shall notify the applicants of its decision. If the decision is favorable, duplicate Certificates of Organization and approved bylaws shall be issued. A certificate of approval authorizing the commencement of business shall be issued upon execution of the certificate of organization and adoption of the bylaws by the organizers and their returning same to the commissioner.

    If it is not favorable, it shall state the reasons therefor. The applicant may request a hearing before the agency within _____ days after mailing a copy of the decision to the applicant. The commissioner, within _____ days after receipt of a request for a hearing, shall set a date therefor at a time and place convenient to the commissioner and the applicants, but not longer than 60 days thereafter.

    If after the hearing the decision is not favorable to the applicant, he may file an appeal upon the record in the court of the county stated in the application as the location for the proposed credit union within 30 days after the date of mailing by certified mail of a copy of the decision to the applicant.

    In the case of an appeal, the agency shall retain the exhibits introduced at the hearing and shall forward them to the court before which the appeal is to be heard. The cost of preparation of the stenographer's record shall be borne by the applicant.

5. Upon issuance of the certificate of approval authorizing the credit union to commence business, the credit union shall be deemed organized under this act.

6. The original certificate of organization and the original bylaws shall be filed in the office of the commissioner. The commissioner shall file a duplicate of the certificate of organization with the clerk of the county in which the credit union will have its place of business. The certificate of approval and a copy of the bylaws approved by the commissioner in writing shall be returned to the credit union.

Credit Union Services

Once the credit union is established, it can provide the following services to meet the needs of its members:

1. Selling or leasing real estate
2. Automated teller machines and electronic funds transfer services
3. Collection activities
4. General personnel services
5. Services used in connection with real estate loan activities (e.g., appraisals and closings)
6. Investment brokerage and management service to an extent not prohibited by law
7. Maintaining an inventory of property available for lease to credit union members
8. Administrative and other services related to commercial loans and participation loans
9. Providing management and operating services
10. Marketing services
11. Sale, lease, or servicing of computer hardware and software
12. Developing and administering individual retirement accounts, Keogh Act, deferred compensation ,and other personnel benefit plans
13. Payroll services.
14. Real estate brokerage services
15. Administering prepaid legal service plans
16. Motor vehicle purchasing services
17. Group travel services
18. Insurance activities to the extent not prohibited by state law

19. Financial services, including financial planning and investment counseling
20. Consumer purchasing referral services
21. Retirement counseling
22. Securities brokerage counselling
23. Estate planning
24. Personal property leasing
25. Service contracts or extended warranty contracts for motor vehicles, motorcycles, recreational vehicles, manufactured homes, boats, computers, or other personal property items

General Powers of Credit Unions

Credit unions have broad powers to benefit its members which shall be stated in its bylaws. The bylaws should cover the power to borrow and make loans and make investments.

Loans

1 Loans to members shall be made subject to the conditions contained in the bylaws. A borrower may repay his or her loan in whole or in part any day the office of the credit union is open for business.

2. Except when the bylaws of a credit union shall otherwise provide, a director, officer, or member of either the credit committee or supervisory committee shall *not* borrow from the credit union in which he or she holds office beyond the amount of his or her holdings in shares and deposits.

3. A credit union, through provisions in its bylaws, at its option, may permit its directors, officers, credit committee members and supervisory committee members to borrow in excess of their shares and deposit holdings on such terms and conditions and in such amounts as the bylaws may permit. A director, officer, credit committee member or supervisory committee member shall not act as a co-maker or endorser for borrowers other than members of his or her immediate family.

4. Loans to directors or members of the credit committee or supervisory committee shall be made in the same manner as are loans to other members, except that the applicant shall not pass on his or her own loan. The aggregate amount of loans to or guaranteed by directors and members of the credit committee and supervisory committee, except to the extent they are secured by a specific

pledge of shares or deposits, shall not exceed 10% of the share capital of a credit union and shall be shown in aggregate as a separate item in the balance sheet of the credit union, and in all reports rendered by the credit union.

5. Upon written application by a member, the credit union may approve a line of credit or other open-end credit agreement, and may grant loan advances to the member within the limit of that open-end credit agreement. If an open-end credit agreement has been approved, an additional loan application shall not be required by this act as long as the aggregate indebtedness does not exceed the approved limit. At its option, the credit union may require re-application for an open-end credit agreement, either periodically or as circumstances warrant.

6. A credit union may participate in loans to credit union members jointly with other credit unions, credit union organizations, or other financial organizations. If a credit union incorporated under this act originates such a loan, it shall retain an interest in the loan of at least 10%.

Investments

1. A credit union may invest funds not used in loans to members in any of the following:

   a. Securities, obligations, or other instruments of or issued by or fully guaranteed as to principal and interest by the United States or any agency or instrumentality of the United States, or in any trust or trusts established for investing directly or collectively in such securities, obligations, or instruments.

   b. The credit union will handle investment securities when in the credit union's prudent judgment, which may be based in part upon estimates which it believes to be reliable, there is adequate evidence that the obligor will be able to perform all it undertakes to perform in connection with the securities, including all debt service requirements, and that the securities may be sold with reasonable promptness at a price which corresponds to their fair value.

   c. The purchase of investment securities in which the investment characteristics are considered distinctly or predominantly speculative, or the purchase of investment securities which are in default, whether as to principal or interest, is prohibited.

   d. As used in this subparagraph, an "investment security" means a marketable obligation in the form of a bond, note, or debenture, commonly regarded as an investment security and which is salable under ordinary circumstances with reasonable promptness at a fair value.

e. Shares or certificates of an open-end management investment company registered with the Securities and Exchange Commission under the Investment Company Act of 1940, Public Law 96-477, 94 Stat. 2275, 2295.

2. A credit union shall not invest more than the amount of its reserves and undivided earnings in any obligor or related obligors except for investments authorized by subsection 1(a) and 1(c) above. This limitation shall not apply to a corporate central credit union.

All these factors suggest that establishing a credit union can be beneficial to the church and its membership. As noted, there must be at least 500 members in order to see the full benefits. The church, as is expected by the application guidelines, must be prepared to show that there are capable persons available to volunteer their time to serve as officers and committee members. A credit union is a functional service that a church should not overlook in addressing the needs of its members.

8

Progressive Ministry Audit

*True progress is moving ahead on one's own accord,
it is not pointing out shortcomings of others.*

*Are you one that can stand up and be counted—
or are you just in the way?*

A church must consider many things when preparing to serve its community. The goals, direction, and organization of the church are extremely important. When these key things are determined, a church can move on to the progressive stage much easier. If a church's objectives are clear and understandable, the congregation will appreciate the effort. The ultimate goal of any church is to please its congregation and satisfy its needs. The church's programs and services must be devised to suit the needs of its members and not its leaders. This may call for changes in the times that services are offered, adding adequate and secured parking, or offering summer and evening programs. A church must be willing to change to make its present members happy. Enacting some changes could also attract new members to the church.

A church must be aware of who its members are to satisfy them more effectively. The church's older population need programs different from that of its younger members. The differences in needs can also be socially caused. For example, a working class church membership body has different needs and expectations than a white collar class of members. Churches must keep the effects of society, money, and its members' environments in mind when attempting to fulfill its members' needs.

Few churches today can survive on faith alone; they also need money. The ways in which a church attempts to gain money should reflect its members' circumstances. Being aware of the economic circumstances of its members will guide a church in effective fundraising.

Efforts to fulfill the needs of members may cause some churches to enact certain changes. These changes may not be easy for some churches to make, but are necessary if the church wants to grow. Being too rigid in its ways will cause a church to lose valuable new members and support from some existing members. The church's leaders must keep this point in mind. If the membership is reluctant to move forward, it may be up to its leader to encourage the members and lead them upon a new path. In a situation where the pastor is reluctant to enact change, the opposite is true. The church members may have to initiate change on their own. No one should be pushed aside to enact change. Everyone should be included if at all possible. This will prevent or alleviate the buildup of possible resentment or contention within the church.

A strong leader is a major factor for this transitional stage. A strong leader can lead a church to success, but strength is not the only quality a leader needs. The church's leader must be willing to share responsibility, and he must be open to suggestions. The leader must also be a visionary to see future possibilities for the church. Not only is a strong leader necessary for success, a good supporting staff is also necessary.

The church's staff reflects upon the church. Outsiders and members alike will judge a church from the actions, attitude, and success of its representatives and staff members. A church must be willing to obtain quality support staff to help the church. Oftentimes a church will have to pay good staff members. Churches should not balk at doing this if the staff members are doing good work which is benefitting the church. The salaries should, however, be reasonable to avoid potential tax problems later.

At this point, a church may wonder, how do we do all these things? There seems to be so much that a church should know or provide that it can be confusing. The situation is actually more simple than it seems. There is a very clear-cut way for churches to discover the information necessary to better serve its members. A church should just ask them!

PROGRESSIVE MINISTRY AUDIT AND CHECKLIST

Here are some suggested questions that church leaders can ask of themselves and their congregations. They should review and study how the questions are answered. The answers will serve as a guide as to how to initiate change and tell the members of the church how much change may be necessary.

Progressive Principle One:
Organization, Outreach, and Community

Note: *Some questions are for the church's leaders and others are for the congregation.*

1. Are the church's programs designed with the congregation's needs in mind?
2. Are members made to feel guilty when told that their participation is needed in church programs and events?
3. Are members encouraged to voice their needs?
4. Are programs designed and planned by the members to fulfill their needs, or is this done by the church's leaders?
5. Is the church's leader aware of the everyday environment of his/her members?
6. Does the church conduct business as if the rules are more important than the members?
7. Is the church's doctrine more important than its relationship with its members?
8. Has there been any major controversy or division in the last five years? If so, what was it?
9. Does the church deal openly with controversy?
10. Do the church's leaders understand the difference between a working Board and an information-gathering Board?
11. For large Boards (25 people or more), is there an executive committee to do the basic work and organization?
12. Can decisions be made within the church without going through a lot of bureaucratic "red tape"?
13. Are most church decisions made according to policy or polity?
14. Are meeting times encouraged to be less than one hour?
15. What is done to aid and support former leaders?
16. Does the church hold a positive image and relationship in the community?
17. How does the church respond to criticism and praise?[89]

Progress Principle Two: Serving Members

1. Is more than one Sunday service offered?
2. If so, does the same minister lead the service?
3. Once a new service is offered, is the church willing to continue offering it?
4. Is the church willing to offer services during the same time as Sunday School?
5. Does the church have a pre-school or grade school?
6. Is a Mother's Day program offered?
7. Are new Sunday School classes implemented every 3-6 months?
8. Is there an adult Sunday School class?
9. Is an evening Sunday service offered?
10. Is a mid-week service or program offered?
11. Is a Bible Study class offered?
12. Are athletic programs available?
13. Does the church have a male or female day?[90]

Progress Principle Three: Growth and Outreach

1. List all monies given to causes outside the congregation in the last 10 years (most recent year first):
2. Do any decreases or increases correspond to a decrease or increase in the congregational size?[91]

Progress Principle Four: Growth and the Public Arena

1. List all programs offered by the church which are social or political in nature such as homelessness, health, disease control, drug/child abuse, AIDS counseling and crime prevention programs in the schools/community.
2. Is the church changing with the times by offering pertinent programs?[92]

Progress Principle Five: Growth That Is Related to Leadership

1. Does the church understand that growth is directly related to its leadership?
2. Does the minister assume a leadership role in the church?

3. What has been the average tenure of a minister over the past 20 years?
4. How long has the present minister been in leadership?
5. Is the church willing to have a minister stay for at least 10 years?
6. Is the church willing to offer vacation time for a minister as an incentive to stay on for a long term?
7. How much vacation time do the minister and staff members presently receive?
8. Is the minister's vision of the church ambitious enough to carry it to growth?
9. Is the minister a leader rather than an enabler?
10. Does the minister initiate change that would otherwise not occur?
11. Does the minister lead the church into topics and areas where it would not otherwise explore?
12. Is the minister able to learn from his mistakes?
13. Is the minister able to delegate power and duties? Does he do so?
14. Does the minister consult with the membership in developing vision for the church's future?
15. Has the minister been able to develop new skills?
16. Is the minister concerned with providing the membership with what it needs, versus what it wants?
17. Is the minister equipped to handle the church's size?
18. Is the church able to evaluate and decide when it is time for a minister to move on?[93]

Progress Principle Six: The Attitude of Staff Members

1. What are the central responsibilities of staff members (to recruit, train, etc.)?
2. Is the church's number of staff members increasing or decreasing?
3. Are programs offered to help staff members develop new skills, both related and functional to their jobs?
4. What are the salaries of the staff members?
   Adequate total salaries:
   0-200 in worship = 60% of total budget
   200+ in worship = 40% of total budget
5. What percentage of the budget is received by staff members?[94]

Progress Principle Seven: Adequate Parking

1. Does the church have enough land? If the church is on less than 8 acres, is there property nearby or adjacent for sale?
2. Has the church recognized and addressed the issue of parking in the last 20 years?
3. What is the average attendance of the most popular service?
4. What is the average number of people per car (in the above situation?
5. Are paved street parking spaces available to members?
6. How much is 80% of the total parking spaces?
7. How many spaces are needed to adequately accommodate the services' attendance?
8. How many spaces need to be added?
9. Do church members have problems finding a parking space during Sunday services?
10. Conclusion: Does the church need more parking?[95]

Progress Principle Eight: Growth Can Occur Even Though a Church Cannot Afford to Build

1. How much would the annual debt be to operate a new facility?
2. What is the present total for the church's indebtedness?
3. What is the ratio of the present debt? (The present debt should not exceed 30% of your total budget.)
4. What would be the ratio of debt if a new facility was added? (This figure should not exceed 33% of the total.)
5. When was the last facility built?
6. Conclusion: Can the church afford the building of a new facility?[96]

Progress Principle Nine: Growth Through Outreach

1. Give a breakdown of who new members have been for the past 10 years (most recent year first).

Same Faith	Other Denomination	Transfer Total

2. Does the church concentrate on new baptisms, transfers or inbreeding of new members' faiths?

3. Does the church intentionally try to reach nondenominational members?
4. How many miles does the average member have to drive to work? How long does it take him?
5. How many miles does the average member drive to reach church service?
6. How many people live near the church?
7. Who are the unchurched people near the church?

    a. Singles never married
    b. Single-parent families
    c. Singles divorced
    d. Young families
    e. Older families
    f. Senior citizens
    g. Upper/Middle/Lower working class families
    h. Ethnic mix

8. Which groups are not being adequately ministered to in the area?
9. Has the population of the congregation increased or decreased over the last 10 years? By how much?
10. Are the schools full in the area of the church?[97]

Progress Principle Ten: Growth Via Courtesy

1. How does the church feel about the parable of the one lost lamb?
2. How many dollars and what percentage of the budget goes to the following forms of advertising?

a. Yellow Pages	$	%
b. Newspaper	$	%
c. Flyers	$	%
d. Radio	$	%
e. Television	$	%
f. Direct Mail	$	%
g. Other	$	%
Total	$	%

Does the total amount represent 5% of the budget?

3. How many families visit each week? Are they contacted within 48 hours?
4. What percentage of families join after visiting the church?
5. What brought these families to the church?

    a. Friends and relatives
    b. Driving by

    c. Newspapers

    d. Yellow Pages

    e. Preschool

    f. Singles within the congregation

    g. Television

    h. Banner

    i. Direct Mail

    j. Other

6. How many contacts are made each week with unchurched people?
7. Does someone on the staff spend twenty hours each week visiting the unchurched?
8. Is it made clear during the worship service that visitors are expected each Sunday?
9. Is every event in the life of the church used as a vehicle for soliciting membership?
10. How many visitors are on the mailing list each week?
11. Are visitors placed on a mailing list the first time they visit.
12. Are Christmas Eve services promoted through adequate space and advertising?
13. Are there adequate exterior and interior signs around the church?
14. Is there an adequate number of trained greeters?
15. Is there an evangelism team?
16. What group of people or segment of the population can be reached to whom no one else is ministering?
17. Is 10% of the parking space designated for visitors?
18. Does the church have a new members' class?
19. Are tours of the facilities provided?
20. When at church, do the members go out of their way to meet and welcome people they do not know?
21. Do the members pray regularly that the church will grow spiritually and numerically?
22. Are information packets provided for visitors?
23. Is the appearance of the church's property pleasing?
24. Conclusion:[98]

Progress Principle Eleven:
Asking for Support Encourages Growth

1. Budeet totals for the past 10 years including operational and debt service which are not income.

2. Is telling people the church needs money avoided, and is talk about members' needs to become stewards normal practice?
3. Does the preparation of the pledge drives involve at least 1/4 of the congregation?
4. Does the leadership understand the importance of pledge Sunday?
5. Is there a pledge drive held every year for budget purposes?
6. Is there at least 3 weeks of education prior to pledging?
7. Does the pledge card ask only for money?
8. What role does the pastor play in the pledge drive?
9. Number of pledges and averages for the past 5 years.

No. of Pledges X Avg. Amount =	Total Pledged Budget	Percent of Budget

10. Do the pledges underwrite more than 70% to 90% of the budget?
11. Have pledges increased or decreased over the years?
12. Based on the record, what kind of income can the church expect next year, if it does nothing differently?

   a. Pledges from new members $
   b. Loose plate $
   c. Regular non-pledgor $
   d. Building-usage fees $
   e. Foundation $
   f. Special offerings $
   g. Sunday school offerings $
   h. Interest $
   i. Memorials $
   j. Other $
   Total $

13. Analysis of last three stewardship programs:
14. Are designated donations encouraged, and a unified budget discouraged?
15. Does the pledge card offer choices?
16. Does the Christmas offering equal at least half of one month's additional income?
17. Is the pledge program personalized?
18. Are there regular special offerings for items within the budget?
19. Does the total budget income (operating and building costs) equal or exceed $1,000 for every person in worship on an average Sunday?

20. Is 1/3 of the church's income derived from more than 1/4 of its pledges?

21.

Total Indebtedness for last 10 Yrs.	Ratio of Indebtedness to Budget.	Budgeted Debt Service Last 10 Yrs.	Ratio of Debt Service to Budget

22.

Budgeted Income Last 10 Yrs.	Ratio of Debt Service to Budgeted Income	Ratio of Indebtedness to Budgeted Income

Note: *Take current year minus first year totals; divide that number by the first year.*

23. Analysis of growth over last 10 years:
    a. Budget growth
    b. Total indebtedness growth
    c. Debt service growth
    d. Budgeted income growth
    e. Congregation growth

24. Breakdown of Current Budget:

19___	Target	Over/Under
Salaries		40%
Debt		25%
Program		10%
Outreach		15%
Advertising		5%
Stewardship		1%

25. List of Financial Resources:
    a. Endowments
    b. Wills
    c. Capital fund pledges
    d. Cash reserves

e. Foundation
f. Stocks and bonds
g. Other
   Total
26. Is there a plan to use this money?
27. Before the mortgage is retired should a new ministry be designated to use that same amount of money?
28. Should the use of plaques be allowed?
29. Should cutting the budget be avoided at all costs?
30. Should new ways of raising money be sought each year?
31. When was the last capital fund drive?
32. Does the pastor know what each member gives?
33. Conclusion:[99]

Progress Principle Twelve:
Long-Term Growth Brings a Solid Foundation

1. Does the church have an overall vision for its ministry and future?
2. Does the church have a mission statement that is clear, concise, and open ended?
3. Does the church have a song or anthem?
4. If so, is it sung consistently?
5. Is there a regularly updated five or ten year plan?
6. Is there a master plan for the use of land and facilities?
7. When was the last time strategic planning was done?
8. What is the church's main strength?
9. What is the church's main weakness?[100]

Progress Principle Thirteen: Regular Strategic Planning
Is Necessary for Healthy Growth

1. Where does the church want to go?
2. Does the church know what it must do now?
3. List present officially adopted objectives/goals of the church.
4. What are the short-term objectives?
5. What are the long-term objectives?
6. Are these objectives people-centered and measurable?
7. Do the objectives of the pastor and the church match?
8. Does the church celebrate when it reaches an objective?
9. Do the objectives keep the church from becoming more interested in numbers than in people?

10. Are there checklists for the objectives?
11. When delegating responsibilities, is the church careful to select people whose skills match the tasks?
12. Are people held accountable?
13. When asking people to do a job, are they informed that the church expects their best?
14. Do the objectives have timeliness?
15. Is each program or strategy evaluated?
16. Is too much time spent setting objectives and not enough time spent implementing them?

Progress Principle Fourteen: Open-Minded for Change

1. Is the church free from power cliques?
2. Do one or two people derail things that the majority wants?
3. Does the church worry too much about hurting people's feelings and not enough about being in ministry?

A Progressive Pastor's Vision

1. Begin the Ministry Audit with a personal assessment of your own attitude toward the mission of the church. Do you have a clear vision of where you want this church to be in twenty years, and are you willing to take it there? Do you believe, and are you willing to act upon the premise that God wants your church to grow and be healthy? The smaller the church, the more important your attitude.
2. If your attitude is right, then no matter what size your church, take a good look at what happens during worship. Is the service relevant? Does the sermon speak to the everyday needs of the person in the pew? Is the music down to earth, easily understood, and lively? Is the space and environment comfortable? Does the bulletin welcome "Joe"? Does your church offer a choice of worship hours?
3. Gather a small group of core leaders who share your vision for the church—people who are objective enough to see beyond their own personal needs. Begin to lead them to discover how they can make the common vision happen in ways that meet their needs.
4. Next, is there an off-street parking space for every two people on the church grounds at peak hours? The larger the church and the

less rural the area, the more important is this ratio. What are your church's actual needs according to the Ministry Audit? Is there land to buy or ground to pave?

5. Make sure your program staff equals one person for every 100 people in worship. There is no point to bringing people in the front door if they go out the back door.
6. Identify a need in your area and fill it. People need a reason to drive to your church if they can just as easily drive across town to a church that meets their needs.
7. If there is a solid mission, are you telling the area about it through advertising and word of mouth? Are you known for the mission throughout the area? Ask your secretary what most calls from the public are regarding.
8. Begin a solid stewardship program of percentage giving and tithing. From the start, let it be known that you personally are a tither and expect others to follow your lead. Do not be afraid to upset people when you talk about money. Remember, for many people, money is their false god.
9. How are you doing with the 80% factor? Do you need to provide additional space? Start with parking, please!
10. Do you add all first-time visitors to your mailing list? Are they contacted within twenty-four hours, and at least four times within the first week after their visit?
11. From here, go with whatever needs the most strengthening and attention. May the grace of God go before you![101]

PASTORAL EMPLOYMENT CONTRACT

Should You Have an Employment Contract?

In our increasing complex society, no longer can the minister be content with employment to a particular church or institution without a written employment contract.

Consider the following example. A young minister is contacted by an out-of-state church and asked to become the pastor. The church orally promises to pay a good salary and fringe benefits, along with paid vacations, and providing a parsonage for the young minister and his family. The congregation has been without a pastor for two years. The congregation votes to hire him as pastor by majority vote. The church bylaws are dated and never followed. The trustee Board makes all the financial decisions for the church—without the knowledge or consent of the membership. The trustee Board is controlled by the chairman, who commands loyalty through the use of money and friendship. The congregation consists of mostly elderly parishioners, not actively involved in the financial affairs of the church. The church and the minister orally agree that the young minister shall be the church's new pastor. The young minister resigns his current good paying job as a professor of theology, and moves his family out of state to become the pastor of the church.

For the first six months, the new pastor and the church get along fine. The new pastor gradually implements new ways of doing things. These changes threaten the power of the trustee Board and especially the chairman. Alarmed, the chairman starts a campaign to remove the new pastor. With the aid of a few Board members and a few church members, the chairman starts false rumors about the pastor. While the majority of the congregation sits on the side lines, not wishing to cross the chairman of the trustee Board, the trustee Board terminates the pastor. As a result, the new pastor is discharged from his position. The Board goes to court and obtains a permanent restraining order barring the young minister from entering the church. The trustees evict the minister and his family from the church parsonage. They cut off his salary and health care benefits. His wife is expecting their fourth child in two weeks and must be hospitalized to insure a safe delivery. Having exhausted all his savings to move and having sold his own home, the young minister is left to solve his problems as best he can.

After prayer, the young minister seeks legal counsel. His lawyer advises that he has little or no chance of winning in court because it will be his word against the church. In addition, because of the publicized affairs of well-known ministers such as Jim Bakker, the court probably will not be very sympathetic.

If you think this kind of thing does not happen in real life, think again. The majority of these facts are taken from a true case. How can you prevent this from happening to you and your family?

This section discusses steps to be taken to reduce your risk of unjust dismissal. This discussion is not meant to be exhaustive, and you are encouraged to seek competent legal counsel prior to entering into any employment contract.

Establishing an Employment Contract

For legal purposes, a church is an employer and you are an employee of the church. Many African-American congregational style churches have little if any written rules or operating procedures. When they do, they are usually outdated and poorly drafted. To protect both you and the church, a written employment contract should be drafted. The contract should be as clear as possible and detail each party's legitimate expectations and responsibilities.

Avoiding Wrongful Discharge

At the beginning of an employment relationship, with expectations high for success, the last thing the parties usually think about is possible discharge. You, however, should insist on a written employment contract that spells out grounds and procedures for discharge. You should insist on language which states that during the term of the employment contract you can only be discharged for good cause. Your duties and responsibilities, salary and benefits package all should be clearly defined. Equally important, is the length of your employment. For example, will your employment be for one year, two years, or indefinitely? I recommend language such as the following:

> The minister shall hold his position for as long as he desires. He can only be discharged for good cause and by majority vote of the congregation at a duly held special church meeting.

The goal is to prevent the minister from becoming an at-will employee who can be discharged for any reason. In most states, employment, unless otherwise stated, is at-will. An employee may be terminated at any time and for any reason. The above language prevents creation of an at-will employment relationship.

Second, the procedure for discharge should be clear, especially if the church bylaws or constitution are silent in this regard. For example, language should be included in the contract such as the following:

> The Rev. Good Shepherd shall not be terminated as pastor during the term of this employment except for good cause. All allegations which form the basis for discharge must be stated in writing. Rev. Good Shepherd shall be notified of the charges against him by certified mail not less than 30 days prior to any disciplinary action. A neutral body made up of ministers and/or lay persons shall be established by the church to determine the merits of the charges. Rev. Good Shepherd shall be allowed to select a person of his choice to be a member of the body and the church shall be allowed to select a party of its choice. The two individuals then shall choose the third member of the investigating committee.
>
> The committee shall investigate the charges and issue a written report to each party within 30 days. A copy of the written report shall be provided to the congregation. At a duly held special church meeting, Rev. Good Shepherd shall be allowed to refute the allegations. The congregation shall vote whether or not to discharge Rev. Good Shepherd. A

majority of the congregation must vote in favor of discharge for said decision to be effective. The congregation must have objective good cause for discharge.

If discharged, Rev. Good Shepherd shall, at a minimum, receive his salary and all other benefits for twelve months as severance pay. Thereafter, Rev. Good Shepherd shall remain on the church's health insurance policy for 24 months and he shall be responsible for payment of any premiums necessary to maintain an active policy. The foregoing is not intended to foreclose Rev. Good Shepherd's right to other legal relief.

The important thing to remember when accepting a new position is to clearly define both the pastor and the congregation's expectations and avoid leaving yourself without legal remedy if wrongfully discharged.

9

Progressive Clergy Checklists

Don't Inspect; Don't Expect!

For years, many churches have enjoyed a tax-exempt status. However, there are some strict guidelines that regulate the exercise of such a privilege. The following checklists are designed to highlight the methods of enforcement used by the IRS and to avoid unnecessary tax problems in planning for the areas of televangelism and gospel production.

CHECKLIST FOR AVOIDING CHURCH AUDITS

1. Be familiar with proper IRS inquiry procedures:
   a. IRS must provide written notice of intent to begin inquiry 15 days before it is to start.
   b. Notice must include the reason for inquiry and an explanation of the Code provision granting the authority to the "administrative and constitutional" provisions of the inquiry.
   c. IRS must provide a description of any activities or records to be examined, a copy of all documents collected in connection with the inquiry, and an offer to set up a conference with the church (if a church elects to schedule a conference within 15 days, the IRS is prohibited from examining church records until after the conference).

2. File the required tax return.
3. Comply with tax withholding requirements for income, FICA (Social Security), and SECA (Self-Employment Contributions Act).
4. Provide information for Cumulative List of Organizations described in Section 170(c) of the Internal Revenue Code of 1954.
5. Supply confirmation that a specific business is or is not owned or operated by the church.
6. Pay taxes on income generated from income-producing activities if:
   a. The income is produced from a trade or business,
   b. The trade or business is continued on a regular basis,
   c. The operation of such trade or business is not substantially related to the church's exempt purpose.
7. Do not provide personnel with excessive compensation (reasonable compensation is the amount that would normally be necessary in a like circumstance).

CHECKLIST FOR THE SELF-EMPLOYED CLERIC

1. Use Schedule C to deduct all business expenses (if taxpayer fails to use Schedule C, then only unreimbursed employees business expenses are deductible as miscellaneous itemized deductions to the extent that they exceed the percent limitation of adjusted gross income indicated by IRS Codes) .
2. Health care deductions. A self-employed cleric is entitled to deduct a percentage of health insurance amounts paid on behalf of himself, his spouse, and dependents prescribed in 1992.
   a. No health care deductions are allowed when the deduction exceeds the individual's net earnings from self-employment.
   b. The self-employed cleric is eligible to participate in a subsidized health plan provided by his/her spouse's employer.
   c. The self-employed cleric provides health insurance for all employees in trades or businesses of which the cleric owns less than 5 percent.
   d. Computation of the amount of income subject to self-employment taxes.
   e. Retirement plan. The self-employed cleric must submit his own separate qualified retirement plan.

3. Health care deductions. An employed cleric may exclude his employer's contributions to the employee health plan from his income.

4. Retirement plan. The church or agency may provide an employed cleric with a qualified retirement plan.

CHECKLIST FOR PARSONAGE DEDUCTION

1. Payments related to renting or providing a home. The following expenditures are directly related to renting or providing a home and are also excludable:

   a. Rent of a home or apartment;

   b. Down payment and mortgage installment payments on a home and related expenses such as real estate commissions, attorney's fees, escrow fees, etc.;

   c. Mortgage interest, real estate taxes and special assessment for such purposes as streets, sewers, etc., regardless of whether they were paid for out of a housing allowance;

   d. Utilities—electricity, water, gas, etc.;

   e. Garbage removal;

   f. Repairs and maintenance;

   g. Home insurance coverage for fire, theft, and accident liability; and

   h. Home furnishings.

2. Rental allowance. Rental allowance paid to a minister may be excluded under the following circumstances:

   a. Minister who does not own a home. When a minister does not own a home but receives part of pay, the allowance is excludable to the extent that:

      (1) The rental allowance is used to rent or provide a home;

      (2) The rental allowance is not more than reasonable compensation for the services performed.

   b. Minister homeowner. A minister who owns his own home and receives a rental allowance as a part of his pay may exclude from gross income the lowest of the following amounts:

      (1) The amount actually used to provide a home,

      (2) The amount officially designated as a rental allowance, or

      (3) The fair rental value of the home including furnishings, utilities, garage, etc.

3. Parsonage allowance. Parsonage allowance may be excluded provided that it can be proven that the allowance was used

    a. For the rental of a home,

    b. For the purchase of a home, or

    c. For expenses relating to maintaining a home other than expenses for food and servants.

4.   Income amounts from out-of-town churches. A traveling evangelist may exclude income received from out-of-town churches for evangelistic services to the extent that the amounts are:

    a. Designated by the host churches as rental allowances, and

    b. Actually used to maintain a permanent home.

CHECKLIST FOR UNRELATED BUSINESS INCOME

1. Has the church obtained the services of a tax attorney?
2. Has the church applied for tax-exempt status? Was the application IRS Form 1023 501(c)(3)approved? This is important because UBI income taxation only applies to tax-exempt organizations.
3. Is the church engaged in any activities that are "carried on for the production of income from the sale of goods or the performance of services"? Is income derived from these activities? (If yes, then the church is engaged in a trade or business).
4. If the answer was "yes" to question number 3, is this trade or business conducted on a regular or continual basis (e.g., weekly)?
5. If the answer was "yes" to question number 3, is this trade or business substantially related to the church's tax-exempt purpose that has been filed with the IRS?

If the church answers "yes" to questions 2–5 then it is probably engaged in UBI producing activities, and it could jeopardize its tax-exempt status, unless the ten principle exceptions are applicable as cited in chapter 3 on tax planning.

6. Is the income from question 3 investment income (income derived from an investment in property, e.g., real estate)?
7. Does the church own 80% of the investment property?
8. Is the income from question 3 derived from debt-financed property (e.g., real estate or securities)?
9. Does the church use the land, at least 85%, in ways substantially related to its tax-exempt function?
10. Are rents received from any property that the church owns?
11. If the answer to question 10 is yes, is this property debt-financed, leased with personal property, or is rental based on a percentage of

the net income derived from the property? If so, then the rent is considered UBI.

12. Has the church received a gain or loss from the sale or exchange of property? If so, it is excluded from tax except in relation to:

    a. Debt-financed property, or

    b. Property classified as inventory or property held primarily for sale in the ordinary course of business.

13. Was a gain realized from the termination of an option to buy or sell securities?

14. Is any income derived from advertisement sold or conducted by the church designed to support the organizations exempt purpose? This income is not taxable.

15. Does the church receive income from bingo games that it conducts in accordance with local laws?

16. Does the church gain income from exchanging or selling it's membership lists to other tax-exempt organizations?

17. Does the church produce income from hosting/organizing conventions, fairs, or trade shows? Are these conventions related to the church's tax-exempt function? If so, the income is not taxable.

CHECKLIST FOR FUND-RAISING

1. What are the church's general goals?
2. What are the church's needs (programs, repair, etc.)?
3. How much does the church need to raise to fulfill its needs?
4. What is the fund-raising program's goal?
5. How have past fund-raising efforts been evaluated and refined?
6. Are monetary donations tax deductible? (Generally, yes, if the church is tax-exempt. If the church is not tax-exempt, gaining this status could help contributions.)
7. What are some of the needs of the targeted potential contributors?
8. What methods of fund-raising will the church use? (They may be used in combinations.)

    a. Tithes

    b. Capital campaign

    c. Memorial gift

    d. Honor gift

    e. Grant

    f. Large donations

9. How will potential donors be contacted? (Several techniques may be used per fund-raising effort.)
   a. Newsletter
   b. Direct Mail
   c. Interviews (phone/in person)
   d. Phone calls
10. How much will contacting potential donors cost?
11. How often will potential donors be contacted?
12. Does the method of contact demonstrate/display how donor's needs and values will be satisfied?
13. Is the donation request personalized?
14. Will donors receive thank-you notes or gifts by mail or personal delivery?

CHECKLIST FOR SENIOR CITIZEN HOUSING

1. Set up a separate 501(c)(3) entity independent of the church.
2. Separate bylaws.
3. Separate board of trustees and directors.
4. What type of housing project will be built?
5. How much will it cost to acquire the land for the project?
6. How much will building construction cost (including planning and design)?
7. What will proposed furnishings and interior designing cost? (The construction must include handicap accessible entrances, hook style door handles, wide hallway corridors, and other features to make the building more user friendly to seniors.)
8. How much will construction of each individual unit cost?
9. Total cost of building senior citizen housing (add 1–3).
10. How much will administrative costs be?
11. What financing entities have been contacted (federal government, local government, state government, and banks)?
12. How much financing can be obtained?
13. What services (including social) will be provided or offered to senior residents?
14. How often will each service be offered (e.g., food service twice daily, entertainment once weekly)?
15. How much will it cost to offer these services? Compute the cost of offering each service individually.
16. Will the added cost be passed on to residents? If so, how?

17. How much will it cost residents monthly to live in this housing project?
18. What will be the criteria for determining who should be allowed to live in the project? Federal government funding is oftentimes linked to who resides in the project.
19. Is there enough demand to fill the units of the project?
20. Identify a team to undertake the project.

    a. Lawyer,
    b. Developer/general contractor,
    c. Accountant.

CHECKLIST FOR GOSPEL MUSIC RECORDING

1. What is the budget for the project (including recording time, expenses, etc.)?
2. Who will be the talent?
3. How will they be compensated?
4. Which method will the church follow?

    a. Demo tape/record deal
    b. Independent production

5. How much will studio time cost (hourly)?

    a. Fee for an engineer
    b. Any other fees for dubbing, overdubbing

6. How many copies of the demo tape are needed? What are the costs?

Method One

1. What record labels will be contacted?
2. Who are the appropriate representatives for each of the above?

    a. Names
    b. Phone numbers
    c. Office addresses

3. Has the record label representative been contacted?
4. Are all demo tapes labeled correctly?

    a. Names of the artists included
    b. Phone numbers and addresses
    c. Titles of the songs and their timing
    d. Lyrics to the songs

5. What other material will be included in the package (biographies, photos, etc.)?

6. How will the package be delivered?
7. Who will contact the label representative in 10–14 days after the package is sent? Is contact made?
8. What was the response? What can be learned from it?
9. Acquire the services of an attorney before signing contracts.

Method Two

1. What will be the cost of recording a master tape?
2. Where can the records, cassettes, and compact discs (CDs) be made? How much will it cost?
3. How much of the product will initially be made?
4. How much will packaging and distribution cost?
5. Which record stores will carry the product?
6. Which radio station managers or programmers will be contacted to get air time?

Publishing

1. Have the songs been selected?
2. Is there an agreement between the church and the songwriter?
3. Has the church copyrighted the songs?
4. Is there a printing company or place to print the songs?
5. How will the songs be marketed?

   a. To record labels
   b. To independent artists
   c. For internal use

6. Has an attorney been consulted?

CHECKLIST FOR CORPORATE SPONSORSHIP

1. What is the planned event? Be specific. Provide:

   a. Date
   b. Time
   c. Place
   d. Cost/Budget

2. Has an attorney been consulted regarding the current tax laws? If so, what are these laws?
3. List the potential sponsors of the event:

   a. Name
   b. Product
   c. Audience
   d. Needs

e. Past sponsored events

f. Amount given in the past

4. How would sponsoring the event fulfill the corporation's needs?

5. How is the event linked to the product? Will sponsoring the event help the corporation reach its target audience or a new group?

6. How many sponsors (from question 3) seem attractive for the event?

7. Who is the appropriate contact person for the corporation?

8. Who will present the proposal to the corporate officials? Do we know the event and company thoroughly?

9. Will the presentation be in a language familiar to the corporation? Is it targeted to appeal to the deciding parties?

CHECKLIST FOR DRUG TREATMENT/OUTREACH PROGRAMS

1. Is there a need for a drug treatment or counseling program in the church's community?

2. Roughly how many addicts are in the area?

3. What space is available for the program?

4. What is the church's basic philosophy?

5. What is its philosophy for the program?

6. Which type of program is best suited for the church's and community's needs, and the church's means?

7. What will be the program's objectives?

8. What specifically will be the program?

9. Who will be the program participants?

   a. Children

   b Teens

   c. Adults

10. What drugs will the program address?

    a. Alcohol

    b. Narcotics

    c. Marijuana

    d. Over the counter

    e. Others

11. Will the program be in-house or out-patient? How long will the program last?

12. What is the program's budget?

13. Who will be the staff members? What is their educational level? Salaries?

    a. Drug treatment program
    b. Drug counseling program
    c. Any former drug addicts

14. How will the program be financed?

    a. Donations
    b. Hospital/clinic affiliation
    c. Fees from patients/addicts
    d. Health insurance of patients/addicts
    e. Federal/state funding

CHECKLIST FOR DAY-CARE CENTER

1. Is there a community need for a day-care center?
2. What is the economic climate of the community?
3. What are the needs of the children and parents in the community?
4. Is funding available to start a day-care center?
5. What are the State Department of Social Services requirements for licensing or regulation of day-care centers?
6. Can the church feasibly fulfill them?
7. Who are the staff members?

    a. Trained/Licensed
    b. Degreed
    c. Volunteers

8. What will be the criteria for selecting the staff (education, experience, etc.)?
9. Which age group(s) will the day-care center serve?

    a. Infant
    b. Toddler
    c. Pre-school
    d. School-aged

10. How many children will be allowed into the center's program?
11. What will be the adult per child ratio?
12. Where will the center be located? How much space per square foot is available?
13. What programs will be offered to the children?

    a. Educational
    b. Physical
    c. Field Trips

    d. Art/music
    e. Food service
    f. Transportation
    g. Tutorial

14. What will be the cost of each offered activity?
15. How much will parents be charged for day-care services weekly?
16. How will the center be funded?

    a. Government funding
    b. Fees to parents
    c. Contributions

17. How will the church evaluate the day-care center's success and initiate changes?

CHECKLIST FOR FOOD CO-OPERATIVES

1. Is your church situated in an area that would benefit from or utilize a food co-op?
2. Have the members of the congregation expressed a concern with the high prices of food in supermarkets?
3. Has the congregation demonstrated a desire and willingness to establish and run a food co-op?

Establishing a Food Co-Operative: The How-To's

1. Determine the objectives of the food co-op.

    a. To save money
    b. To get better food
    c. To help others

2. Determine whether to incorporate.

    a. How many members are involved?
    b. How much capital has been acquired?
    c. Is the membership constant?
    d. Is the lifetime of the operation fixed or indefinite?

3. Determine whether to incorporate as a non-stock or stock co-op.
4. Draft the Articles of Incorporation and Bylaws.
5. Complete state form for incorporation:

    a. State name of food co-op
    b. State purpose or function of entity
    c. Identify resident agent
    d. Identify resident agent's office address
    e. Identify the names of the incorporators

6. Submit Articles of Incorporation to the appropriate state agency with nominal fee.
7. Draft bylaws. Include provisions governing
   a. Management and director conduct
   b. Bookkeeping requirements
   c. Periodic audits
   d. Voting rights
8. Does your home state impose a state sales tax on food?

   Check with the state sales tax department or the state public welfare division for procedures on how to secure a state tax-exempt certificate.
9. Does your group wish to become authorized to accept food stamps?
   a. Incorporate as a nonprofit organization
   b. File Form 1023 Application for federal tax-exempt status
   c. Secure a state tax-exempt certificate from the appropriate state agency
   d. Secure certificate from city health inspector's office
   e. Present certificates to the USDA Food Stamps Office
   f. Receive authorization card or license renewable annually

Preliminary Practical Matters of Forming a Food Co-operative

1. Conduct research on types of food to purchase.
2. Devise methods for selecting foods to buy.
3. Research available food sources.
4. Obtain pricing information:
   a. Size of bulk order
   b. Bulk quantity that foods are available
   c. Determine business hours
   d. Acceptable method of payment
   e. Availability of delivery service
   f. When payment is due
   g. Refund policy
   h. Means of acquiring information on products
5. Obtain necessary people/equipment:
   a. Drivers
   b. Loaders
   c. Scales
   d. Storage facilities

  e. Lighting

  f. Easily cleanable floors

  g. Close proximity to food sources and members

  h. Broom

  i. Pencils

  j. Marking pens

  k. Tape

  l. Scissors

  m. Used egg cartons

  n. Bags

  o. Dustpans;

6. Designate official mailing address.
7. Determine frequency of purchases.
8. Determine frequency of meetings.

CHECKLIST FOR CHURCH AND COMMUNITY DEVELOPMENT CORPORATIONS

The Composition of Community Development Corporations

Authoritative Body

1. Has a Board of Directors been selected to establish a broad operational policy of organization?
2. How many people sit on the Board of Directors?
3. Does the Board of Directors represent a broad cross-section of the church community?
4. Are the Directors likely to be active participants in directing the focus and development of the organization?
5. How financially solvent is the organization?
6. If the organization is financially strong, the CDC should appoint an Executive Director to handle the daily responsibilities of the CDC such as stabilizing funding and implementing Board policy.
7. Has the organization begun to grow?
8. If so, should staff be added?
9. If not, the Board of Directors should divide the organization's responsibilities among themselves.

Structure of Community Development Corporations

The model of a CDC varies depending upon whether the church is focused on

1. Neighborhood revitalization
2. Economic development
3. Job training

The Planning Process

1. Establishing your CDC Mission
2. Acquiring and developing the skills necessary to undertake your CDC project
3. Determining your organizational structure and tax status
4. Identifying your venture
5. Developing your business plan
6. Seeking financial support
7. Building and maintaining community support and involvement

Developmental Strategy

The following list identifies some of the areas in which you may need skilled persons to accomplish your developmental strategies:

1. Community organization
2. Legal advice
3. Accounting
4. Financial packaging and financial planning
5. Grantsmanship
6. Marketing and advertising
7. Personnel management
8. Land acquisition/property management
9. Architecture
10. Business planning
11. Public relations
12. Construction
13. Strategic planning

The Focus of Various CDC Organizations: Neighborhood Revitalization

A church may direct the focus of its CDC toward neighborhood revitalization upon consideration of the following:

1. Is the church located in close proximity with dilapidated structures?
2. Do the church members have access to materials and supplies that they can donate to further the cause?
3. Does the church membership include skill tradesmen who will donate their labor to make repairs?

Job Training

1. Is the church considering becoming involved in neighborhood revitalization?
2. Do the church members have skilled trades where there are traditionally not a large minority representation?
3. Is there an adult education program which offers training in such trades in the vicinity of the church?
4. Are there enough skilled tradesmen in the congregation to create a private corporation to provide similar services to the CDC for profit?

Venture Capital

1. Venture capital is a risky undertaking for CDC that should not be pursued without considering the following factors:
   a. Are there members with strong financial training and background?
   b. Does the CDC have a large capital base to take risk?

Benefits to the Church

A church can benefit from forming a CDC in a number of the following ways:

1. Expands the outreach efforts of the church to persons beyond the sanctuary.
2. Improves the quality of the church.
3. Provides financial benefits to a church as an alternate means of fundraising.
4. Enhances church membership.

CHECKLIST FOR CREDIT UNION FORMATION

1. Submit application.
   a. Name and location of proposed credit union.
   b. Names and addresses of organizers:
      (1) Minimum of seven (7)
      (2) All must be residents of Michigan

       (3) Number of shares subscribed (if any)

   c. Application fee must be paid.

2. Secure approval.

   a. Criteria for approval:

       (1) Proposed credit union would benefit its members

       (2) Deposits (shares) insured by NCUA

       (3) Proposed credit union is consistent with the purposes of the Michigan Credit Union Act

       (4) Discretion of the Commissioner

   b. Certificate of Organization and Bylaws issued upon approval.

   c. Certificate of Approval issued upon execution of Certificate of Organization and adoption of Bylaws by organizers.

3. Body Corporate (upon issuance of the Certificate of Approval).

4. Meet minimum capital requirements (shall consist of member share accounts).

5. If denial of application occurs:

   a. Applicant may request a hearing within 30 days after mailing of decision;

   b. Hearing must be scheduled within 10 days after receipt of request for hearing;

   c. Hearing must be held within 60 days after receipt of request for a hearing;

   d. Appeal to the circuit court of the county where the proposed credit union is to be located, or to the court of local jurisdiction within 30 days after mailing of hearing decision.

6. Adopt fiscal year (shall end December 31).

10

Forms

The wise is never grown, regardless of age, but continues to grow.

CONSTITUTION AND BYLAWS

Preamble

Whereas the Holy Scriptures 1 Corinthians 14:40 admonishes us to do all things in the Church decently and in order, therefore, we hereby do adopt this Constitution to determine the discipline and the rules according to which the affairs of this congregation shall be conducted and its temporalities administered.

Article 1—Name

The corporate name of this Church, a nonprofit ecclesiastical corporation, shall be _____ , Inc., and the term of the existence of this corporation shall be perpetual.

Article 2—Doctrinal Platform

The doctrinal platform of this Church shall be The Holy Bible, as it is the inerrant, infallible Word of God.

Article 3—Church Covenant

Having been led, as we believe, by the Spirit of God, to receive the Lord Jesus Christ as our Savior, and on the profession of our faith, having been baptized in the name of the Father, and of the Son, and of the Holy Ghost, we do now, in the presence of God, angels, and this assembly, most solemnly and joyfully enter into this covenant with one another, as one body in Christ.

We engage, therefore, by the aid of the Holy Spirit, to walk together in Christian love; to strive for the advancement of this Church in knowledge, holiness, and comfort; to promote its prosperity and spirituality; to sustain its worship, ordinances, discipline, and doctrines; to contribute cheerfully and regularly to the support of the ministry, the expenses of the Church, the relief of the poor, and the spread of the gospel through all nations.

We further engage to watch over one another in brotherly love; to remember each other in prayer; to aid each other in sickness and distress; to cultivate Christian sympathy in feeling and courtesy in speech; to be slow to take offense, but always ready for reconciliation, and mindful of the rules of our Savior, to secure it without delay.

And now unto Him who brought again from the dead Our Lord Jesus be Power and Glory forever. Amen.

Article 4—Purpose

The purpose of this local Church shall be to:

(1) Seek the salvation of the lost, through the preaching of the Gospel of Christ: Psalms 125:4, 5; Proverbs 11:30; Matthew 4:15; Mark 16:15, 16; Luke 14:23; John 20:21; Acts 1:8; Romans 1:16, 10:14; 1 Corinthians 1:18–21;

(2) Adhere to the preaching of the Gospel for the reproof, rebuke, and exhortation of the saints: 1 Timothy 5:20; 2 Timothy 4:2; Titus 2:15;

(3) Promote Christian fellowship: 1 John 1:3–7.

Article 5—What We Believe: Eighteen Articles of Faith

1. Of the Scriptures

We believe that the Holy Bible was written by men divinely inspired and is a perfect treasure of heavenly instruction; that it has God for its author, salvation for its end, and truth without any mixture of error for its matter; that it reveals the principles by which God will judge us; and, therefore, is and shall remain to the end of the world, the true center of Christian union and the supreme standard by which all human conduct, creeds, and opinions should be tried.

2. Of the True God

We believe that there is one, and only one, living and true God, an infinite intelligent Spirit, whose name is Jehovah, the Maker and Supreme Ruler of heaven and earth; inexpressibly glorious in holiness, and worthy of all possible honor, confidence, and love; that in the unity of the Godhead, there are three persons, the Father, the Son, and the Holy Ghost; equal in every divine perfection, and executing distinct but harmonious offices in the great work of redemption.

3. Of the Fall of Man

We believe that man was created in holiness, under the law of his Maker, but by voluntary transgression fell from that holy and happy state; in consequence of which all mankind are now sinners, not by restraint, but choice; being by nature utterly void of the holiness required by the law of God, positively inclined to evil; and, therefore, under just condemnation to eternal ruin, without defense or excuse.

4. Of Justification

We believe that the great gospel blessing which Christ secures to such as believe in him is Justification; that Justification includes the pardon of sin and the promise of eternal life on principles of right-eousness; that it is bestowed, not in consideration of any works of right-eousness which we have done, but solely through faith in the Redeemer's blood; by virtue of which faith his perfect righteousness is freely imputed to us of God; that it brings us into a state of most blessed peace and favor with God, and secures every other blessing needful for time and eternity.

5. Of Grace in Regeneration

We believe that in order to be saved, sinners must be regenerated or born again; that regeneration consists in giving a holy disposition to the mind; that it is effected, in a manner about our comprehension, by the power of the Holy Spirit in connection with divine truth, so as to secure our voluntary obedience to the gospel; and that its proper evidence appears in the holy fruits of repentance and faith and newness of life.

6. Of God's Purpose of Grace

We believe that Election is the eternal purpose of God, according to which he graciously regenerates, sanctifies, and saves sinners; that being perfectly consistent with the free agency of man, it comprehends all the means in connection with end; that it is a most glorious display of God's sovereign goodness, being infinitely free, wise, holy, and unchangeable; that it utterly excludes boasting, and promotes humil-ity, love, prayer, praise, trust in God, and active imitation of his free mercy; that it encourages the use of means in the highest degree; that it may be ascertained by its effects in all who truly believe the gospel; that it is the foundation of Christian assurance; and that to ascertain it with regard to ourselves demands and deserves the utmost diligence.

7. Of a Gospel Church

We believe that a visible Church of Christ is a congregation of bap-tized believers, associated by covenant in the faith and fellowship of the gospel; observing the ordinances of Christ; governed by His laws; and exercising the gifts, rights, and privileges invested in them by His work; that its only Scriptural officers are Bishops or Pastors, and Deacons, whose qualifications, claims, and duties are defined in the epistles to Timothy and Titus.

8. Of Baptism and the Lord's Supper

We believe that Christian Baptism is the immersion in water of a believer, into the name of the Father, and Son, and Holy Ghost; to show forth, in a solemn and beautiful emblem, our faith in the crucified, buried, and risen Savior, with its effect in our death to sin and resurrection to a new life; that is prerequisite to the privileges of a Church relation; and to the Lord's Supper; in which the members of the Church, by the sacred use of bread and wine, are to commemorate together the dying love of Christ; preceded always by solemn self-examination.

God's Plan of Church Finance

God nowhere in His Word says that His Churches are to have sales, raffles, or bazaars to raise money for their work. God does not want His children to be beggars, going out in the world asking for means to carry on.

God gives only one plan of Church finance in the Bible, and that is TITHES and OFFERINGS from His people. Therefore, we as believers in Christ, will NEVER engage in sales, raffles, teas, fashion shows, bazaars, or the like as a means of receiving finances for our Church.

Our only means of receiving monies will be through TITHES and OFFERINGS. The tithe is the tenth, meaning that God's people are to bring a tenth of their incomes to the Lord and His work. Offerings are the amounts that are given above the tenth. This is the plan that God teaches all through His Word, and it is the one scriptural plan of Church finance, thus the one we do hereby adopt.

(Genesis 14:20, 28:22; Numbers 18:21–28; Leviticus 27:30; 2 Chronicles 31:5–12; Malachi 3:8–10; Matthew 5:20, 23:23; Luke 11:42; 1 Corinthians 9:12, 14; 1 Corinthians 16:2; Hebrews 7:8)

Article 6—Powers

This Church may hold real estate, franchises, and own property, and may borrow money and issue bonds or other evidences of indebtedness, and to sure the same, may execute mortgages or deeds of trust upon its property for the acquisition or improvement of any real estate or other property which may be acquired or held by it for the purpose aforesaid.

The congregation shall have the supreme power and control and custody of all its real and personal property, temporalities, and revenues, and the administration of its ecclesiastical affairs, in accordance with God's Word, subject to the provisions of the Articles of Incorporation and to the Constitution and Bylaws of the Church.

Article 7—Membership

The membership of this congregation shall at all times consist of persons who have:

(1) Believed and confessed the Lord Jesus Christ as the only begotten Son of God and Savior of the world:

    (a) Candidate for Baptism: Mark 16:16;

    (b) Christian Experience: providing said person has been baptized according to the doctrines of this Church;

    (c) By Letter: when membership is being transferred from another Baptist Church; and

    (d) Restoration: when said person pledges faithfulness: 1 Corinthians 4:2

(2) Been baptized in the name of the Father, and of the Son, and of the Holy Ghost: Matthew 28:19.

(3) Been accepted into this membership/Christian fellowship: Acts 2:47.

(4) Been registered ANNUALLY in the Church office, according to procedures given by the Pastor.

(5) Completed all orientational procedures as directed by the Pastor.

In order for an accepted Member to become a Voting Member, he/she MUST:

(1) Be a born-again believer in Christ who has reached the age of accountability:

(2) Be a regular supporter of the financial/giving program of Tithes and Offerings: Malachi 3:8–10; Matthew 23:23; 2 Corinthians 9:6–8.

(3) Be a regular attendant of Worship Services: Hebrews 10:25; Sunday School: 1 Timothy 2:15; and a partaker of the Lord's Supper: 1 Corinthians 11:17–34.

Members having voting privileges shall be entitled to vote when present in person at any business meeting of the membership called for the purpose of voting on any issue with respect to which a vote is required as provided in this Constitution. Voting Members shall not be entitled to vote by proxy, and there will be no SECRET BALLOT VOTING allowed at this Church. Except as may otherwise specifically provided herein, the vote of a majority of Voting Members present at any business meeting of the membership shall be binding upon the Church.

Membership in this Church may be suspended or terminated by:

(1) Letter of dismissal or transfer;
(2) Dropping from membership roll for:
    (a) Failure to contribute;
    (b) failure to attend worship services, Sunday School, and the Lord's Supper;
    (c) causing discord/division amongst the membership, i.e., instituting a court case/suit against the Pastor and/or Church: Proverbs 6:16–19; Matthew 18:15–19; Romans 16:27.

If any Member shall fail to abide by Articles 3, 4, 5, and 8 of this Constitution, or should such a Member be suspended or expelled (Romans 16:17; Matthew 18:15–19; 1 Corinthians 6:12) or fail to commune for a two (2) month period of time (1 Corinthians 11:17–34) or fail to financially contribute for a three (3) month period of time (Malachi 3:8–10; Matthew 23:23; Acts 20:35; Luke 6:38; 1 Corinthians 16:2; 2 Corinthians 9:6–8), then all voting rights and any and all other privileges and all offices bestowed upon said Member shall, without any action of the congregation, immediately become null and void and of no effect, in other words, said Member loses the privileges of membership, automatically, in this Church.

Any Voting Member of this Church who neglects to attend Sunday School, worship services, and/or the observance of the Lord's Supper of this Church for any consecutive two (2) months or for the same length of time fails to contribute of his/her means to support the ministry and Church shall be urged by the Pastor and Deacons to return to duty. If he/she fails to do so, following the third (3rd) consecutive month, his/her name shall be transferred automatically from the active (voting) membership roll to the inactive (non voting) membership roll. Illness and age are exceptions only in the event that the Pastor is notified, and passes his approval.

The mechanism for members moving from the inactive to the active membership roll shall be determined by the Pastor.

Article 8—Officers

The officers of this church shall be:

PASTOR—He is the general overseer (Acts 20:28), undershepherd (1 Peter 4:2–4), and physical authority (Hebrews 13:17) of the Church. He is responsible for the Annual Calendar of Church Events and for the selection of the Annual Days and Promotional Sundays. He is the chief executive officer of the Church, the caller and moderator of ALL meetings, and the executive official leader of ALL auxiliaries, and may call them together at any time. He has full charge of all choirs. The Pastor shall determine the agenda for all meetings. The Pastor, without vote of the members or of the Trustees, hires all Church personnel: music staff, clerical staff, and custodial staff. The Pastor shall determine the number of staff members, their job duties, days and hours of employment, titles and salaries, and may terminate their employment at his discretion. The Pastor has full charge of the pulpit, and only the Pastor has the privilege to offer it to any other minister or layman. The Pastor is in charge of ALL services at the Church, and they will be directed by him. All services held in the name of _____ Church, whether held on the Church premises or away from the Church premises, MUST be approved by the Pastor. All officers and leaders shall in all cases be appointed by the Pastor. The Pastor shall have the power to silence and/or expel any Member who is not found in accord with the guidelines of Matthew 18:15–19; 1 Corinthians 6:1, 2; Romans 16:17; and/or the rules herein contained. The Pastor shall visit the sick and have them visited by an associate, when called upon, whether confined in the home or hospital (James 5:14). All expenses incurred by the Pastor and all other Church personnel for this purpose shall be reimbursed by the Church.

OFFICIAL PRESENTATION—The Pastor is vested by the Voting Members with absolute authority to officially represent the Members of the Church in all matters relating to the Church, which representation is binding upon the Church. In this official capacity, the Pastor is accountable and amenable to the Voting Members only.

The Pastor is vested with full authority to designate the depository or depositories in which funds of the Church may be deposited from time to time and against which demand for withdrawal may be made, and to designate officials of the Church whose signatures will be required for the withdrawal of funds, to endorse notes, to endorse drafts, to execute mortgage notes and deeds, to serve as guarantors or otherwise by their signatures pledge the assets of the Church for obligations of the Church.

The Pastor shall be called by a majority vote of the eligible Voting Members (see Article 8) present at a special meeting of the Members in Conference as directed by the Holy Spirit; Jeremiah 3:15; John 14:26. A special meeting called for the purpose of electing a Pastor must be announced in the Church Sunday morning worship services on no less than two (2) consecutive Sundays.

The Pastor shall serve the Church for an indefinite period, since there is no scriptural support of tenure. (Exodus 16:33–35). The compensation of the Pastor shall be determined from time to time by the vote of the Board of Trustees; provided, that the Pastor shall abstain from voting on matters relating to his compensation.

The Church shall also be responsible for the maintenance of the Pastor's home and grounds, paying all utility bills, lawn maintenance, snow removal expenses and any other expenses incurred in the upkeep of the parsonage. The Church shall also be responsible for a certain amount of money for the care of the Pastor's car and other necessities connected with his work.

The Church shall also pay the premiums on health care insurance for the Pastor, his spouse, and any dependent children under eighteen (18) years old, automobile insurance on the Pastor's car, homeowner's insurance on the parsonage, life insurance on the Pastor, disability insurance, and a retirement policy on the Pastor.

If the Pastor should become disabled to carry on his work, he shall be paid his full salary as long as the Voting Members agree to the same, provided he has served for no less than fifteen (15) years. The provisions of the retirement and disability insurance shall lessen the financial responsibilities of the Church for this purpose.

If the Pastor should die while in the service of the Church, the Church shall bear his funeral expenses and shall give his widow his full salary for three (3) months.

If, at any time, the Church shall become dissatisfied with the services of the Pastor and asks for his resignation (Psalm 105:15; 1 Chronicles 16:22), the congregation, at that time, shall take a vote and be governed by the majority vote of Voting Members eligible under the guidelines of Article 8. If the majority votes against the Pastor, the Church, at that time, shall pay the Pastor six (6) months salary in advance or his services shall continue until such time as the Church shall meet this requirement.

In the event the membership becomes dissatisfied with the Pastor, a two-thirds (2/3) vote of the total Voting Membership determined as provided under Article 8 will be required to force the Pastor's resignation. The house will be polled prior to voting, and the vote taken will be a STANDING VOTE.

If, at any time, the Pastor shall become dissatisfied or for any reason desire to resign, he shall be held responsible to the Church for three (3) months, if the Church votes to accept his resignation, or for six (6) months if they vote not to receive his resignation.

DEACONS—The Deacons are the helpers of the Pastor (Acts 6:1–7) and are accountable to the Pastor. The Pastor will deem appropriate the number of Deacons to constitute the deaconship of this Church. Because the Deacons are accountable to the Pastor, they are to be appointed and approved by the Pastor. Their tenure, however long or short, shall be determined by the Pastor, and can be terminated by the Pastor for the following reasons:

(1) Failure to attend Sunday School (2 Timothy 2:15), Worship Services (Hebrews 10:25), and/or the Lord's Supper (1 Corinthians 11:17–34), or to contribute financially (1 Corinthians 16:2); or

(2) Being guilty of spreading malicious gossip (Acts 6:3; 1 Timothy 3:8–11), and/or causing division amongst Church parishioners (Romans 16:17), or insubordination to the Pastor (Hebrews 13:170).

The Deacons, as those appointed to give assistance to the Pastor, are to visit those who are sick and shut-in and to sit in council with the Pastor in spiritual matters. The Deacons will meet at a time called/designated by the Pastor.

The Chairman and co-chairman of the deaconship will be appointed by the Pastor. Any Deacon(s) found meeting in houses to discuss Church business shall automatically be removed from the deaconship. Any meeting held without the presence of the Pastor shall be of NO EFFECT.

During any interim period when the Church is without a Pastor, whether by reason of death, resignation or severing of the Church/ Pastor relationship, it is incumbent upon the chairman of Deacons to call together the Deacons at the earliest possible date for the following:

(1) To nominate a Pulpit Committee of seven (7) Voting Members whose duty shall be to supply the pulpit with a Fundamental Missionary Baptist Minister to deliver a gospel message when the same is required;

(2) Nominate, on an interim basis, a regular ordained Fundamental Missionary Baptist Minister to be in charge of the pulpit taking care of the regular order of services whose duties shall end at the completion of that task;

(3) Establish a date of a business meeting at which all nominations and recommendations of the Pulpit Committee shall be approved, altered, or rejected by the Voting Members of the Church. In the case the Voting Members reject part or

all of the nominations from the Pulpit Committee, the Voting Members shall have the authority to nominate and elect a Pastor from the floor.

Moreover, it shall be the duty of the Deacons to assemble the members of the Church together in a business meeting to establish a time when the Church shall elect a Pastor and to give guidance to the Church in electing a Pastor.

The Deacons shall have such other duties as may be assigned to them from time to time by the Pastor and as are elsewhere described in this Constitution and Bylaws.

TRUSTEES—The management of the affairs of this congregation shall be vested in the Pastor working with TRUSTEES, which shall number ten (10), not including the Pastor. The Pastor, by virtue of his position, shall automatically be a voting member of the Board of Trustees. All other Trustees shall be appointed by the Pastor. They shall:

(1) Serve for one year, unless sooner removed by the Pastor for:

    (a) Failure to attend worship services (Hebrews 10:25), Sunday School (2 Timothy 2:15), or the Lord's Supper (1 Corinthians 11:17–34);

    (b) Failure to contribute financially (Malachi 3:8–10; 1 Corinthians 16:2);

    (c) Causing division (Matthew 18:15–19; Romans 16:17; 1 Corinthians 6).

(2) Have a chairman, co-chairman, and secretary that will be appointed by the Pastor;

(3) Have charge of the property of the Church with emphasis on its physical upkeep;

(4) Along with the Deacons, constitute a Finance Committee that shall count and deposit all funds received by the Church in a bank;

(5) Give written reports to the membership drafted under the supervision of the Pastor;

(6) Along with two (2) Deacons, two (2) Trustees, and the Pastor, constitute a Budget Committee that shall draft the Annual Proposed Budget for the current expenses of the Church; and

(7) Invest all funds given or bequeathed to this Church, if any, paying particular attention to the terms of the gift or bequest as to any specifications of the use of the income. If

no specific rules are given, the money shall be disbursed according to a vote of the Voting Members of the Church.

Any Trustees found meeting in houses to discuss Church business shall automatically be removed from the Board of Trustees. Any meeting held without the presence of the Pastor shall be of NO EFFECT. Meetings of the Board of Trustees (including joint meetings of the Board of Trustees and the Deacons) will be set at the discretion of the Pastor.

TREASURER—The Treasurer of this Church shall be appointed by the Pastor. The Treasurer shall serve from a term of one (1) year, unless removed by the Pastor, and he shall be eligible to succeed himself. The Treasurer shall be a member of the Board of Trustees and Finance Committee, and, under the direction of the Pastor and Trustees, receive and deposit all monies received by the Church. The Treasurer shall disburse monies according to the Church's dictates whether they be intended for benevolent purposes or for local support.

FINANCIAL SECRETARY—The Financial Secretary of this Church shall be appointed by the Pastor. The Financial Secretary shall serve for a term of one (1) year, unless sooner removed by the Pastor, and he shall be eligible to succeed himself. The Financial Secretary may be a member of the Board of Trustees or Finance Committee and may perform the duties of the Treasurer to the extent authorized by and under the direction of the Pastor and Trustees.

CHURCH CLERK—The Church Clerk shall be appointed by the Pastor and shall serve at his pleasure. The Clerk shall keep an accurate record of the proceedings of all business meetings, sign whatever documents require the Clerk's signature, and report the minutes of the meetings when called upon to do so.

The Treasurer, Financial Secretary and Church Clerk as well as the Deacons and Trustees can be removed from office, without vote of the Church, for failure to attend Worship Services (Hebrews 10:25), Sunday School (2 Timothy 2:15), the Lord's Supper (1 Corinthians 11:17–34) and for failure to contribute financially on a regular basis (Malachi 3:8–10); 1 Corinthians 16:2).

Article 9—Interim Government

If the Pastor shall die, resign or be removed from office in accordance with the provisions of Article 9, the remaining officers of the Church shall continue to serve in their respective capacities as such until the next succeeding Annual Stewardship Meeting of the Church.

In the interim, each successor to the Pastor shall serve in accordance with the provisions of this Constitution and Bylaws, subject, however, to the direction of the Board of Trustees and Deacons, acting jointly as the interim governing body of the Church. At the next succeeding Annual Stewardship Meeting of the Church, the Board of Trustees, together with any proposed alterations or amendments, to the Voting Members of the Church for ratification in accordance with the provisions of Article 13. Thereafter, the Church shall be governed by its Articles of Incorporation and by the Constitution and Bylaws in the form ratified by the Voting Members.

Any vacancy in any office of the Church (other than that of Pastor) which may occur during the period of interim government may be filled by the affirmative vote of a majority of the remaining members of the Board of Trustees and Deacons, acting jointly.

Article 10—Meetings of This Church

WORSHIP ASSEMBLIES—This Church shall meet regularly every Lord's Day (Sunday) for Sunday Church School and Public Worship of the Almighty God; every Wednesday for Mid-Week Services of prayer and thanksgiving; and every First Sunday in the month for Baptism and the observance of the Lord's Supper; the latter shall be evening services.

BIBLE STUDY ASSEMBLIES—Bible Study assemblies will be held at the following times for the promotion of the growth of all believers in Christ in the grace and knowledge of our Lord and Savior Jesus Christ.

Sunday: Sunday Evening Bible Class.

Wednesday: Sunday School Teachers' Meeting. All Sunday School Teachers MUST be present at this meeting if they expect to teach on the upcoming Sunday.

Other Bible study assemblies may be scheduled as designated by the Pastor.

BUSINESS MEETINGS—The members of the Church shall meet annually in December at an Annual Stewardship Meeting, on a date and at a time announced by the Pastor, to receive an account of the business transactions and financial receipts of the Church. The meeting will be announced from the pulpit and published in the weekly Church bulletin for two (2) consecutive Sundays immediately preceding the proposed meeting; provided, however, that if the notice has been given, and it is deemed advisable to postpone the meeting, notice of such postponement shall be given and read from the pulpit and/or published in the weekly Church bulletin every Sunday until the meeting is held.

SPECIAL MEETINGS—Special meetings may be called by the Pastor alone, or along with the Deacons and Trustees, whenever, in their discretion, it is advisable or upon written request of not less than fifty (50) active, eligible Voting Members. Notice of such meeting and its purpose shall be given from the pulpit and/or published in the weekly Church bulletin on the two (2) consecutive Sundays immediately preceding the proposed meeting.

STAFF AND MUSIC COMMITTEE MEETINGS—All Staff Meetings and all meetings of the Music Committee shall be called by the Pastor and held on such dates and at such times as he deems necessary.

Article 11—Auxiliaries and Christian Education Department

Auxiliary units shall be established, the officers of which shall be appointed by the Pastor for a term of one (1) year. All such officers shall have the ability to succeed themselves, and they will serve at the pleasure of the Pastor.

No auxiliary is a banking unit. All monies, if any, must be turned into the Church office. If any such monies are received for benevolent purposes, they will be disbursed by a check written through the Church office.

No person will be allowed to be a member of an auxiliary unit if he fails to attend Sunday School (2 Timothy 2:15; Acts 11:26); Worship Services (Hebrews 10:25); the Lord's Supper (1 Corinthians 11:17–34), or fails to contribute financially (Malachi 3:8–10; 1 Corinthians 16:2). Any auxiliary members that fail to do so will automatically relinquish their auxiliary positions.

The same standards MUST be met by: Junior Church workers, Nursery workers, Sunday School teachers and members of the Board of Christian Education.

Auxiliary units that are presently established:

Choirs
Ushers
Courtesy Guild
Nurses
Deaconesses

No programs, fellowships, picnics, or other activities shall be planned by any unit or group of units of this congregation without the approval of the Pastor. Any unit or group doing so will be dissolved, leader and members, as a unit of this congregation, automatically.

Article 12—Amendments

This Constitution shall not be altered or amended unless proposed alterations or amendments be submitted in writing at any Annual Stewardship Meeting. Any such proposed amendment or alteration must be announced, at the least, on two (2) consecutive Sundays and published in the weekly Church bulletin. A two-thirds (2/3) vote of the Voting Members present shall be necessary for the adoption of such alterations or amendments to any articles or sections of this Constitution. Such alterations or amendments of any article or section shall be inserted herein at length as so altered or amended.

C&S-502 (Rev. 1-84)

MICHIGAN DEPARTMENT OF COMMERCE — CORPORATION AND SECURITIES BUREAU	
(FOR BUREAU USE ONLY)	Date Received
CORPORATION IDENTIFICATION NUMBER	

ARTICLES OF INCORPORATION
For use by Domestic Nonprofit Corporations
(Please read instructions and Paperwork Reduction Act notice on last page)

Pursuant to the provisions of Act 162, Public Acts of 1982, the undersigned corporation executes the following Articles:

ARTICLE I

The name of the corporation is:

ARTICLE II

The purpose or purposes for which the corporation is organized are:

ARTICLE III

The corporation is organized upon a _____ basis.
(stock or nonstock)

1. If organized on a stock basis, the aggregate number of shares which the corporation has authority to issue

    is _____ . If the shares are, or are to be, divided into classes, the designation of each class, the number of shares in each class, and the relative rights, preferences and limitations of the shares of each class are as follows:

ARTICLE III

2. If organized on a nonstock basis, the description and value of its real property assets are: (if none, insert "none")

   and the description and value of its personal property assets are: (if none, insert "none")

   The corporation is to be financed under the following general plan:

   The corporation is organized on a _____ basis.
   (membership or directorship)

ARTICLE IV

1. The address of the registered office is:

   _____ , Michigan _____
   (Street Address) (City) (ZIP Code)

2. The mailing address of the registered office if different than above:

   _____ , Michigan _____
   (P.O. Box) (City) (ZIP Code)

3. The name of the resident agent at the registered office is:

ARTICLE V

The name(s) and address(es) of all the incorporator(s) is (are) as follows:

Name   Residence or Business Address

_____

_____

_____

_____

_____

_____

_____

_____

_____

_____

_____

Use space below for additional Articles or for continuation of previous Articles. Please identify any Article being continued or added. Attach additional pages if needed.

I (We), the incorporator(s) sign my (our) name(s) this _____ day of _____, 19____.

_____   _____

_____   _____

_____   _____

_____   _____

_____   _____

BYLAWS OF COMMUNITY DEVELOPMENT CORPORATION

(A Michigan Nonprofit Corporation)

Article I
Offices

1.01 PRINCIPAL OFFICE. The principal office of the corporation shall be at such place within the State of Michigan as the Board of Directors shall determine from time to time.

1.02 OTHER OFFICES. The corporation may also have other offices at such other places as the Board of Directors from time to time determine or the business of the corporation requires.

Article II
Purpose

2.01 PURPOSE. The purpose(s) for which the corporation is formed are as follows:

A. The purpose of the corporation shall be exclusively educational, charitable, and scientific, within the meaning of Section 501(c)(3) of the United States Internal Revenue Code, as the same may be amended. Subject to that limitation, the corporation is organized and shall be operated to purchase, own and operate apartment building space, which is to be rented at below-cost rates.

Article III
Members

3.01 MEMBERS. The members of the corporation shall be the vestry of Church of the Messiah, an Episcopal church located in Detroit, Michigan.

3.02 VOTING RIGHTS. Each member shall have one vote.

3.03 TERMINATION OF MEMBERSHIP. Any member may resign by submitting a written resignation either at a meeting of the membership or of the Board of Directors or by mailing to the Corporation at its principal office, and thereupon such resignation shall become effective forthwith without need of any acceptance, unless otherwise specified therein. Except as otherwise required by law, any member may be removed from membership by a majority vote of the members cast at any annual meeting or at any special meeting of the members called for that purpose or by a majority vote of the Board of Directors at any regular or special meeting.

3.04 TRANSFER OF MEMBERSHIP. Membership in this corporation is personal and is not transferable or assignable.

Article IV
Meeting of Members

4.01 ANNUAL MEETING. An annual meeting of the members shall be held on the last Sunday during the month of January, beginning with the year 1993, for the purpose of electing directors and for the transaction of such other business as may come before the meeting. If the day fixed for the annual meeting shall be a legal holiday in the State of Michigan, such meeting shall be held on the next succeeding business day. If the election of directors shall not be held on the day designated herein for any annual meeting, or at any adjournment thereof, the Board of Directors shall cause the election to be held at a special meeting of the members as soon thereafter as conveniently possible.

4.02 SPECIAL MEETINGS. Special meetings of the members may be called by the President, the Board of Directors, or not less than one-tenth of the members.

4.03 PLACE OF MEETING. All meetings of members shall be held at the principal office of the corporation or at such other place as shall be determined by the Board of Directors and stated in the notice of meeting.

4.04 NOTICE OF MEETING. Written or printed notice stating the place, day and hour of any meeting of members shall be delivered, either personally or by mail, to each member entitled to vote at such meeting, not less than six nor more than twenty-five days before the date of such meeting, by or at the direction of the president, secretary, or the officers or persons calling the meeting. In case of a special meeting or when required by statute or by these Bylaws, the purpose or purposes for which the meeting is called shall be stated in the notice. If mailed, the notice of meeting shall be deemed to be delivered when deposited in the United States mail addressed to the member at his address as it appears on the records of the corporation, with prepaid postage thereon.

4.05 QUORUM. Members entitled to vote at a meeting who hold fifty-percent (50%) of all the votes which may be cast shall constitute a quorum at such meeting. If a quorum is not present at any meeting of members, a majority of the members present may adjourn the meeting from time to time without further notice.

4.06 ACTION BY MEMBERS IN LIEU OF MEETING. Any action required by law to be taken at a meeting of members may be taken without a meeting if a consent in writing, setting forth the action so taken, shall be signed by four-fifths of the members. Prompt notice shall be given to members who have not consented in writing.

4.07 PROXIES. Voting by proxy shall be permitted at membership meetings. Every proxy shall be in writing, signed by the member and dated, and shall specifically state the particular membership meeting to which it is applicable, but need not be sealed, witnessed, or acknowledged. Any proxy must be filed with the secretary before the appointed time of each meeting.

Article V
Board of Directors

5.01 GENERAL POWERS. The affairs of the corporation shall be managed by its Board of Directors.

5.02 NUMBER, TENURE, ELECTION AND QUALIFICATIONS. The number of directors shall be five (5). Directors need not be members of the corporation. The directors shall be elected by the members at each annual meeting. Each director shall hold office until the next annual meeting of members and until his successor shall have been elected and qualified.

5.03 REGULAR MEETINGS. A regular annual meeting of the Board of Directors shall be held without other notice than this bylaw, immediately after, and at the same place as, the annual meeting of members. The Board of Directors may provide by resolution the time and place for the holding of additional regular meetings of the Board without other notice than such resolution.

5.04 SPECIAL MEETINGS. Special meetings of the Board of Directors may be called by or at the request of the president or any two directors. The person or persons authorized to call special meetings of the Board may fix any place, either within or without the State of Michigan, as the place for holding any special meeting of the Board called by them.

5.05 NOTICE. Notice of any special meeting of the Board of Directors shall be given at least two days previously thereto by written notice delivered personally or sent by mail or telegram to each director at his address as shown by the records of the corporation. If mailed, such notice shall be deemed to be delivered when deposited in the United States mail in a sealed envelope so addressed, with postage thereon prepaid. If notice be given by telegram, such notice shall be deemed to be delivered when the telegram is delivered to the telegraph company. Any director may waive notice of any meeting. The attendance of a director at any meeting shall constitute a waiver of notice of such meeting, except where a director attends a meeting for the express purpose of objecting to the transaction of any business to be transacted at, nor the purpose of, any regular or special meeting, unless specifically required by law of by these bylaws. The time and place of the special meeting shall be stated in the notice.

5.06 QUORUM. A majority of the Board of Directors shall constitute a quorum for the transaction of business at any meeting of the Board; but if less than a majority of the directors are present at said meeting, a majority of the directors present may adjourn the meeting from time to time without further notice.

5.07 MANNER OF ACTING. The act of majority of the directors present at a meeting at which a quorum is present shall be the act of the Board of Directors, unless the act of a greater number is required by law or by these bylaws.

5.08 VACANCIES. Any vacancy in the Board of Directors caused by any reason other than the removal of a director by a vote of the membership shall be filled by a vote of the majority of the remaining directors, even though they may constitute less than a quorum; and each person so elected shall be a director until a successor is elected by the members at the next annual meeting.

5.09 COMPENSATION. Directors as such shall not receive any compensation for their services. Directors shall be reimbursed for expenses incurred while serving as a director when such expense is properly evidenced by a receipt and approved by a majority of the other directors.

5.10 ACTION BY DIRECTORS IN LIEU OF MEETING. Any action required by law to be taken at a meeting of the directors, or any action which may be taken at a meeting of the directors, may be taken without a meeting if a consent in writing, setting forth the action so taken, shall be signed by all of the directors.

Article VI
Officers

6.01 NUMBER. The Board of Directors shall elect or appoint a President, a Secretary, and a Treasurer, and may select one or more Vice-

President, Assistant Secretary and/or Assistant Treasurer. The President and Treasurer shall be members of the Board of Directors. Any two of the above offices, except those of President and Vice-President, may be held by the same person, but no officer shall execute, acknowledge, or verify an instrument in more than one capacity.

6.02 ELECTION AND TERM OF OFFICE. The officers of the corporation shall be elected annually by the Board of Directors at the regular annual meeting of the Board of Directors. If the election of officers shall not be held at such meeting, such election shall be held as soon thereafter as conveniently possible. New offices may be created and filled at any meeting of the Board of Directors. Each officer shall hold office until his successors shall have been duly elected and shall have qualified.

6.03 REMOVAL. Any officer elected or appointed by the Board of Directors may be removed by the Board of Directors by a vote of a majority of all Directors whenever in the judgment of the Board of Directors the best interests of the corporation would be served thereby.

6.04 VACANCIES. A vacancy in any office because of death, resignation, removal, disqualification or otherwise, may be filled by the Board of Directors for the unexpired portion of the term.

Article VII
Duties of Officers

7.01 PRESIDENT. The president shall be the principal executive officer of the corporation and shall, in general, supervise and control all of the business and affairs of the corporation. He shall preside at all meetings of the members and of the Board of Directors. He may sign, with the secretary or any other proper officer of the corporation authorized by the Board of Directors, any deeds, mortgages, bonds, contracts, or other instruments which the Board of Directors has authorized to be executed, except in cases where the signing and execution thereof shall be expressly delegated by the Board of Directors or by these bylaws or by statute to some other officer or agent of the corporation; and in general he shall perform all duties as may be prescribed by the Board of Directors from time to time.

7.02 VICE-PRESIDENT. In the absence of the president or in the event of his inability or refusal to act, the vice president (or in the event there be more than one vice-president, the vice presidents in the order of their election) shall perform the duties of the president and when so acting, shall have all the powers of and be subject to all the restrictions upon the president. Any vice-president shall perform such other duties as from time to time may be assigned to him by the president or by the Board of Directors.

7.03 SECRETARY. The Secretary shall attend all meetings of the Board of Directors and of members and shall record all votes and minutes of all proceedings in a book to be kept for that purpose. He shall give or cause to be given notice of all meetings of the members and of the Board of Directors. He shall keep in safe custody the seal of the corporation, and, when authorized by the Board, affix the same to any instrument requiring it, and when so affixed it shall be attested by his signature, or by the signature of the Treasurer or the Assistant Secretary. The Secretary may delegate any of his duties, powers and authorities to one or more Assistant Secretaries, unless such delegation is disapproved by the Board.

7.04 TREASURER. The Treasurer shall have charge and custody of and be responsible for all funds and securities of the corporation; receive and give receipts for moneys due and payable to the corporation from any source whatsoever, and deposit all such moneys in the name of the corporation in such banks, trust companies or other depositories as shall be selected in accordance with the provisions of the Article VIII of these bylaws; and in general perform all duties as from time to time may be assigned to him by the president or by the Board of Directors. The Treasurer shall also render monthly statements showing the financial condition of the corporation. The Treasurer shall prepare for an audit to be made at least once a year and shall present the report of the audit to the corporation at its annual meeting. The audit shall be conducted by a committee appointed by the Board of Directors or by an accountant retained for that purpose.

7.05 ASSISTANT SECRETARIES AND TREASURERS. The assistant treasurers and assistant secretaries, in general, shall perform such duties as shall be assigned to them by the treasurer or the secretary or by the president or the Board of Directors.

Article VIII
Special Corporate Acts

8.01 ORDERS FOR PAYMENT OF MONEY. All checks, drafts, notes, bonds, bills of exchange and orders for payment of money of the corporation shall be signed by such officer or officers or such other person or persons as the Board of Directors may from time to time designate.

8.02 CONTRACTS AND CONVEYANCES. The Board of Directors of the corporation may in any instance designate the officer and/or agent who shall have authority to execute any contract, conveyance, mortgage, or other instrument on behalf of the corporation, or may ratify or confirm any execution. When the execution of any instrument has been authorized without specification of the executing officers or agents, the President or any Vice-President, and the Secretary or Assistant Secretary or Treasurer or Assistant Treasurer, may execute the same in the name and on behalf of this corporation and may affix the corporate seal thereto.

8.03 DEPOSITS. All funds of the corporation shall be deposited from time to time to the credit of the corporation in such banks, trust companies or other depositories as the Board of Directors may select.

8.04 GIFTS. The Board of Directors may accept on behalf of the corporation any contribution, gift, bequest, or devise for the general purpose or for any special purpose of the corporation.

Article IX
Books and Records

9.01 BOOKS AND RECORDS. The corporation shall keep accurate and complete books and records of all accounts and shall also keep minutes of the proceedings of its members, Board of Directors, and committees having any of the authority of the Board of Directors and shall keep at the registered or principal office a record giving the names and addresses of the members entitled to vote. All books and records of the corporation may be inspected by any member, or his agent or attorney for any proper purpose at any reasonable time.

Article X
Fiscal Year

10.01 FISCAL YEAR. The fiscal year of the corporation shall begin on the first day of January and end on the last day of December in each year.

Article XI
Seal

11.01 SEAL. The Board of Directors shall provide a corporate seal, which shall be in the form of a circle and shall have inscribed thereon the name of the corporation, which seal shall be in the charge of the Secretary.

Article XII
Waiver of Notice

12.01 WAIVER OF NOTICE. Whenever any notice is required to be given under the provisions of the Michigan Non-Profit Corporation Act or under the provisions of the articles of incorporation or the bylaws of the corporation, a waiver thereof in writing signed by the person or persons entitled to such notice, whether before or after the time stated therein shall be deemed equivalent to the giving of such notice.

Article XIII
Dissolution

13.01 DISSOLUTION. Upon dissolution of the corporation, no member shall be entitled to any distribution or division of the corporation's remaining money and property, or the proceeds thereof, and the Board of Directors shall distribute all remaining money and property, after paying or making provisions for payment of all debts and obligations of the corporation, in furtherance of the charitable purposes set forth in Article II, that such organization or organizations which are at the time of dissolution qualified as tax-exempt under Section 501(c)(3) of the Internal Revenue Code or the corresponding provisions of any future United States Revenue Law, as the Board of Directors shall determine. Any such assets not so disposed of shall be disposed of by the appropriate court for such charitable purposes exclusively and to such organizations exclusively.

Article XIV
Amendments

14.01 AMENDMENTS. These bylaws may be altered, amended, or repealed, and new bylaws may be adopted by the vote of three or more of the directors at any regular or special meeting or by the vote of two-thirds of the members present at any regular or special meeting of the members, provided, however, that the directors shall have no power to alter, amend or repeal or adopt new bylaws relating to the number, term of office, or powers of the directors.

RESOLUTIONS RELATING TO BORROWING AND LENDING

1. Resolutions of Board of Trustees authorizing officers to borrow money

RESOLVED, That the officers of this Church be and they hereby are authorized and directed to borrow, in behalf of this Church, from such banks or trust companies as they may in their judgment determine, an amount not exceeding _____ ($ _____) Dollars, for such period of time and upon such terms and rate of interest as may to them in their discretion seem advisable, and to execute notes in respect thereto in the name of the Church for the payment of the amount so borrowed.

2. Resolutions of Board of Trustees authorizing Church to borrow from officer and to execute note as evidence of obligation.

WHEREAS, the Board of Trustees deems it advisable and necessary for the Church to borrow the sum of $ _____($ _____) Dollars to meet current obligations, and

WHEREAS, in view of the present market conditions, the Church finds itself unable to raise the same sum except upon the payment of an exorbitant premium, and

WHEREAS, _____ , President of this Church, has indicated his willingness and ability to lend the said sum of _____ ($ _____) Dollars to the Church for a period of _____ (___) years, at a low rate of interest,

NOW, THEREFORE, BE IT RESOLVED, That this Church borrow the said sum of _____ ($ _____) Dollars from _____ , its President, and that the Treasurer of this Church be and he hereby is authorized and directed to execute and deliver to the said _____ , President of this Church, a note in the amount of _____ ($ _____) Dollars, payable in _____ (_____) years with interest at the rate of _____ (_____ %) per cent per annum.

3. Resolution of Board of Trustees authorizing officers to borrow money from a named bank, and to execute a mortgage on real property as security therefor.

RESOLVED, That the officers of this Church be and they hereby are authorized, empowered, and directed to borrow the sum of _____ ($ _____) Dollars from the _____ Bank at _____ (_____ %) per cent interest, for a period of _____ years, and to execute as security for said loan a first mortgage on the real property of the Company, situated (insert description of the property to be mortgaged), and to do such other things and to execute such other documents as may be necessary and proper to effect the foregoing.

4.   Resolution of directors authorizing employment of finance company to sell bonds issued under mortgage, and making provision for compensation.

RESOLVED, That the Vice-President of this Church be and he hereby is authorized to employ the _____ Trust Company to sell, for the account of this Church, at not less than par and accrued interest, each and all of the bonds authorized to be issued under the mortgage to be executed by this Church, to the _____ Trust Company and _____ , as Trustees, and to pay to said Trust Company, as compensation for its services in selling said bonds, an amount equal to _____ (_____ %) per cent of the principal amount of the bonds so sold.

FORMATION OF A CREDIT UNION

The undersigned _____ (Complete Name) Credit Union, Inc. _____ (Complete address), a credit union, operating under the credit union law of the State of _____ claims exemption from federal income tax and supplies the following information relative to its operation:

1) Date of incorporation:_____.
2) It was incorporated under the credit union laws of the State of _____ and is being operated under uniform bylaws adopted by said state.
3) In making loans, the State Credit Union Law requirements including their purposes, security, and rate of interest charged thereon, are complied with.
4) Its investments are limited to securities which are legal investments for credit unions under the State Credit Union Law.
5) Its dividends on shares, if any, are distributed as prescribed by the State Credit Union Law.

I, the undersigned, a duly authorized officer of the _____ Credit Union, Inc., declare that the above information is a true statement of facts concerning the Credit Union.

Dated:_____   _____

                                     Authorized Representative

Read the instructions for each Part carefully.

A User Fee must be attached to this application.

If the required information and appropriate documents are not submitted along with Form 8718 (with payment of the appropriate user fee), the application may be returned to you.

Complete the Procedural Checklist on page 7 of the instructions.

Part I   **Identification of Applicant**

1a Full name of organization (as shown in organizing document)

2 Employer identification number (If none, see instructions.)

1b c/o Name (if applicable)

3 Name and telephone number of person to be contacted if additional information is needed

1c Address (number, street, and room or suite no.)

(   )

1d City or town, state, and ZIP code

4 Month the annual accounting period ends

5 Date incorporated or formed

6 Activity codes (See instructions.)

7 Check here if applying under section:

a ☐ 501(e)   **b** ☐ 501(f)   **c** ☐ 501(k)

8 Did the organization previously apply for recognition of exemption under this Code section or under any other section of the Code? . . . .   ☐ Yes ☐ No
If "Yes," attach an explanation.

9 Is the organization required to file Form 990 (or Form 990-EZ)? . . . .   ☐ N/A ☐ Yes ☐ No
If "No," attach an explanation (see instructions).

10 Has the organization filed Federal income tax returns or exempt organization information returns? . .   ☐ Yes ☐ No
If "Yes," state the form numbers, years filed, and Internal Revenue office where filed.

11 Check the box for the type of organization. BE SURE TO ATTACH A CONFORMED COPY OF THE CORRESPONDING DOCUMENTS TO THE APPLICATION BEFORE MAILING (See **Specific Instructions, Part I, Line 11.**) Get Pub. 557, **Tax-Exempt Status for Your Organization, for examples of organizational documents.)**

a ☐ Corporation—Attach a copy of the Articles of Incorporation (including amendments and restatements) showing approval by the appropriate state official; also include a copy of the bylaws.

b ☐ Trust—Attach a copy of the Trust Indenture or Agreement, including all appropriate signatures and dates.

c ☐ Association— Attach a copy of the Articles of Association, Constitution, or other creating document, with a declaration (see instructions) or other evidence the organization was formed by adoption of the document by more than one person; also include a copy of the bylaws.

If the organization is a corporation or an unincorporated association that has not yet adopted bylaws, check here ▶ ☐

I declare under the penalties of perjury that I am authorized to sign this application on behalf of the above organization and that I have examined this application, including the accompanying schedules and attachments, and to the best of my knowledge it is true, correct, and complete.

Please Sign Here ▶

_____ _____ _____
(Signature)   (Title or authority of signer)   (Date)

For Paperwork Reduction Act Notice, see page 1 of the instructions.   Cat. No. 17133K

Part II   Activities and Operational Information

1   Provide a detailed narrative description of all the activities of the organization—past, present, and planned. **Do not merely refer to or repeat the language in the organizational document.** Describe each activity separately in the order of importance. Each description should include, as a minimum, the following: (a) a detailed description of the activity including its purpose; (b) when the activity was or will be initiated; and (c) where and by whom the activity will be conducted.

2   What are or will be the organization's sources of financial support? List in order of size.

3   Describe the organization's fundraising program, both actual and planned, and explain to what extent it has been put into effect. Include details of fundraising activities such as selective mailings, formation of fundraising committees, use of volunteers or professional fundraisers, etc. Attach representative copies of solicitations for financial support.

Part II Activities and Operational Information *(Continued)*

4 Give the following information about the organization's governing body:

a Names, addresses, and titles of officers, directors, trustees, etc.	**b** Annual compensation

c Do any of the above persons serve as members of the governing body by reason of being public officials or being appointed by public officials? . . . . ☐ Yes ☐ No
If "Yes," name those persons and explain the basis of their selection or appointment.

d Are any members of the organization's governing body "disqualified persons" with respect to the organization (other than by reason of being a member of the governing body) or do any of the members have either a business or family relationship with "disqualified persons"? (See **Specific Instructions, Part II, Line 4d.**). . . . . ☐ Yes ☐ No
If "Yes," explain.

5 Does the organization control or is it controlled by any other organization? . . . . ☐ Yes ☐ No

Is the organization the outgrowth of (or successor to) another organization, or does it have a special relationship with another organization by reason of interlocking directorates or other factors? . . . . ☐ Yes ☐ No
If either of these questions is answered "Yes," explain.

6 Does or will the organization directly or indirectly engage in any of the following transactions with any political organization or other exempt organization (other than a 501(c)(3) organization): **(a)** grants; **(b)** purchases or sales of assets; **(c)** rental of facilities or equipment; **(d)** loans or loan guarantees; **(e)** reimbursement arrangements; **(f)** performance of services, membership, or fundraising solicitations; or **(g)** sharing of facilities, equipment, mailing lists or other assets, or paid employees? . . . . ☐ Yes ☐ No
If "Yes," explain fully and identify the other organizations involved.

7 Is the organization financially accountable to any other organization? . . . . ☐ Yes ☐ No
If "Yes," explain and identify the other organization. Include details concerning accountability or attach copies of reports if any have been submitted.

Part II **Activities and Operational Information** *(Continued)*

8 What assets does the organization have that are used in the performance of its exempt function? (Do not include property producing investment income.) If any assets are not fully operational, explain their status, what additional steps remain to be completed, and when such final steps will be taken. If "None," indicate "N/A."

9 Will the organization be the beneficiary of tax-exempt bond financing within the next 2 years?. . . . ☐ **Yes** ☐ **No**

10a Will any of the organization's facilities or operations be managed by another organization or individual under a contractual agreement?. . . . . ☐ **Yes** ☐ **No**

b Is the organization a party to any leases? . . . . ☐ **Yes** ☐ **No**
If either of these questions is answered "Yes," attach a copy of the contracts and explain the relationship between the applicant and the other parties.

11 Is the organization a membership organization? . . . . ☐ **Yes** ☐ **No**
If "Yes," complete the following:

a Describe the organization's membership requirements, and attach a schedule of membership fees and dues.

b Describe the organization's present and proposed efforts to attract members, and attach a copy of any descriptive literature or promotional material used for this purpose.

c What benefits do (or will) the members receive in exchange for their payment of dues?

12a If the organization provides benefits, services, or products, are the recipients required, or will they be required, to pay for them? . . . . ☐ **N/A** ☐ **Yes** ☐ **No**
If "Yes," explain how the charges are determined, and attach a copy of the current fee schedule.

b Does or will the organization limit its benefits, services, or products to specific individuals or classes of individuals? . . . . ☐ **N/A** ☐ **Yes** ☐ **No**
If "Yes," explain how the recipients or beneficiaries are or will be selected.

13 Does or will the organization attempt to influence legislation?. . . . . ☐ **Yes** ☐ **No**
If "Yes," explain. Also, give an estimate of the percentage of the organization's time and funds that it devotes or plans to devote to this activity.

14 Does or will the organization intervene in any way in political campaigns, including the publication or distribution of statements? . . . . ☐ **Yes** ☐ **No**
If "Yes," explain fully.

Part III   Technical Requirements

1   Are you filing Form 1023 within 15 months from the end of the month in which your organization was
    created or formed? . . . .   ☐ **Yes** ☐ **No**
    If you answer "Yes," do not answer questions on lines 2 through 7.

2   If one of the exceptions to the 15-month filing requirement shown below applies, check the appropriate box and proceed
    to question 8.
    Exceptions—You are not required to file an exemption application within 15 months if the organization:

    ☐ **a** Is a church, interchurch organization of local units of a church, a convention or association of churches, or an
             integrated auxiliary of a church (see instructions);
    ☐ **b** Is not a private foundation and normally has gross receipts of not more than $5,000 in each tax year; or

    ☐ **c** Is a subordinate organization covered by a group exemption letter, but only if the parent or supervisory organization
             timely submitted a notice covering the subordinate.

3   If the organization does not meet any of the exceptions on line 2, are you filing Form 1023 within 27
    months from the end of the month in which the organization was created or formed? . . . .   ☐ **Yes** ☐ **No**

    If "Yes," your organization qualifies under section 4.01 of Rev. Proc. 92-85, 1992-42 I.R.B. 32, for an
    automatic 12-month extension of the 15-month filing requirement. Do not answer questions 4 through 7.

    If "No," answer question 4.

4   If you answer "No" to question 3, has the organization been contacted by the IRS regarding its failure to
    file Form 1023 within 27 months from the end of the month in which the organization was created or
    formed? . . . .   ☐ **Yes** ☐ **No**

    If "No," your organization qualifies for an extension of time to apply under the "reasonable action and
    good faith" requirements of section 5.01 of Rev. Proc. 92-85. Do not answer questions 5 through 7.

    If "Yes," answer question 5.

5   If you answer "Yes" to question 4, does the organization wish to request relief from the 15-month filing
    requirement? . . . .   ☐ **Yes** ☐ **No**

    If "Yes," give the reasons for not filing this application prior to being contacted by the IRS. See Specific
    Instructions, Part III, Line 5, before completing this item. Do not answer questions 6 and 7.

    If "No," answer question 6.

6   If you answer "No" to question 5, your organization's qualification as a section 501(c)(3) organization can
    be recognized only from the date this application is filed with your key District Director. Therefore, do you
    want us to consider the application as a request for recognition of exemption as a section 501(c)(3)
    organization from the date the application is received and not retroactively to the date the organization
    was created or formed? . . . .   ☐ **Yes** ☐ **No**

7   If you answer "Yes" to the question on line 6 above and wish to request recognition of section 501(c)(4) status for the period
    beginning with the date the organization was formed and ending with the date the Form 1023 application was received (the
    effective date of the organization's section 501(c)(3) status), check here ▶ ☐ and attach a completed page 1 of Form 1024
    to this application.

Part III   **Technical Requirements** *(Continued)*

8   Is the organization a private foundation?
☐ **Yes** (Answer question on line 9.)
☐ **No**   (Answer question on line 10 and proceed as instructed.)

9   If you answer "Yes" to the question on line 8, does the organization claim to be a private operating foundation?
☐ **Yes** (Complete Schedule E)
☐ **No**

After answering the question on this line, go to Part IV.

10 If you answer "No" to the question on line 8, indicate the public charity classification the organization is requesting by checking the box below that most appropriately applies:

THE ORGANIZATION IS NOT A PRIVATE FOUNDATION BECAUSE IT QUALIFIES:

a	☐	As a church or a convention or association of churches (CHURCHES MUST COMPLETE SCHEDULE A.)	Sections 509(a)(1) and 170(b)(1)(A)(i)
b	☐	As a school (MUST COMPLETE SCHEDULE B.)	Sections 509(a)(1) and 170(b)(1)(A)(ii)
c	☐	As a hospital or a cooperative hospital service organization, or a medical research organization operated in conjunction with a hospital (MUST COMPLETE SCHEDULE C.)	Sections 509(a)(1) and 170(b)(1)(A)(iii)
d	☐	As a governmental unit described in section 170(c)(1).	Sections 509(a)(1) and 170(b)(1)(A)(v)
e	☐	As being operated solely for the benefit of, or in connection with, one or more of the organizations described in **a** through **d**, **g**, **h**, or **i** (MUST COMPLETE SCHEDULE D.)	Section 509(a)(3)
f	☐	As being organized and operated exclusively for testing for public safety.	Section 509(a)(4)
g	☐	As being operated for the benefit of a college or university that is owned or operated by a governmental unit.	Sections 509(a)(1) and 170(b)(1)(A)(iv)
h	☐	As receiving a substantial part of its support in the form of contributions from publicly supported organizations, from a governmental unit, or from the general public.	Sections 509(a)(1) and 170(b)(1)(A)(vi)
i	☐	As normally receiving not more than one-third of its support from gross investment income and more than one-third of its support from contributions, membership fees, and gross receipts from activities related to its exempt functions (subject to certain exceptions).	Section 509(a)(2)
j	☐	The organization is a publicly supported organization but is not sure whether it meets the public support test of block **h** or block **i**. The organization would like the IRS to decide the proper classification.	Sections 509(a)(1) and 170(b)(1)(A)(vi) or Section 509(a)(2)

If you checked one of the boxes a through f in question 10, go to question
15. If you checked box g in question 10, go to questions 12 and 13.
If you checked box h, i, or j, go to question 11.

Part III   **Technical Requirements** *(Continued)*

11   If you checked box **h, i,** or **j** on line 10, has the organization completed a tax year of at least 8 months?
☐ Yes—Indicate whether you are requesting:
☐ A definitive ruling (Answer questions on lines 12 through 15.)
☐ An advance ruling (Answer questions on lines 12 and 15 and attach two Forms 872-C completed and signed.)
☐ No—**You must request an advance ruling by completing and signing two Forms 872-C and attaching them to the application.**

12   If the organization received any unusual grants during any of the tax years shown in Part IV-A, attach a list for each year showing the name of the contributor; the date and the amount of the grant; and a brief description of the nature of the grant.

13   If you are requesting a definitive ruling under section 170(b)(1)(A)(iv) or (vi), check here ▶ ☐ and:

  a Enter 2% of line 8, column (e) of Part IV-A _____
  b Attach a list showing the name and amount contributed by each person (other than a governmental unit or "publicly supported" organization) whose total gifts, grants, contributions, etc., were more than the amount entered on line **13a** above.

14   If you are requesting a definitive ruling under section 509(a)(2), check here ▶ ☐ and:

  a For each of the years included on lines 1, 2, and 9 of Part IV-A, attach a list showing the name of and amount received from each "disqualified person." (For a definition of "disqualified person," see **Specific Instructions, Part II, Line 4d.**)
  b For each of the years included on line 9 of Part IV-A, attach a list showing the name of and amount received from each payer (other than a "disqualified person") whose payments to the organization were more than $5,000. For this purpose, "payer" includes, but is not limited to, any organization described in sections 170(b)(1)(A)(i) through (vi) and any governmental agency or bureau.

15 Indicate if your organization is one of the following. If so, complete the required schedule. (Submit only those schedules that apply to your organization. **Do not submit blank schedules.**)	Yes	No	If "Yes," complete Schedule:
Is the organization a church?			A
Is the organization, or any part of it, a school?			B
Is the organization, or any part of it, a hospital or medical research organization?			C
Is the organization a section 509(a)(3) supporting organization?			D
Is the organization a private operating foundation?.			E
Is the organization, or any part of it, a home for the aged or handicapped?			F
Is the organization, or any part of it, a child care organization?.			G
Does the organization provide or administer any scholarship benefits, student aid, etc.?			H
Has the organization taken over, or will it take over, the facilities of a "for profit" institution? . . .			I

Part IV   Financial Data

Complete the financial statements for the current year and for each of the 3 years immediately before it. If in existence less than 4 years, complete the statements for each year in existence. **If in existence less than 1 year, also provide proposed budgets for the 2 years following the current year.**

A. Statement of Revenue and Expenses

		Current tax year	3 prior tax years or proposed budget for 2 years			
		(a) From .... to	**(b)** 19.......	**(c)** 19........	**(d)** 19........	**(e) TOTAL**
Revenue	1 Gifts, grants, and contributions received (not including unusual grants—see instructions). . .					
	2 Membership fees received . .					
	3 Gross investment income (see instructions for definition) . .					
	4 Net income from organization's unrelated business activities not included on line 3					
	5 Tax revenues levied for and either paid to or spent on behalf of the organization					
	6 Value of services or facilities furnished by a governmental unit to the organization without-charge (not including the value of services or facilities generally furnished the public without charge)					
	7 Other income (not including gain or loss from sale of capital assets) (attach schedule) . .					
	8 **Total** (add lines 1 through 7)					
	9 Gross receipts from admissions, sales of merchandise or services, or furnishing of facilities in any activity that is not an unrelated business within the meaning of section 513					
	10 **Total** (add lines 8 and 9) . .					
	11 Gain or loss from sale of capital assets (attach schedule). . .					
	12 Unusual grants.					
	13 **Total** revenue (add lines 10 through 12)					
Expenses	14 Fundraising expenses . . .					
	15 Contributions, gifts, grants, and similar amounts paid (attach schedule)					
	16 Disbursements to or for benefit of members (attach schedule) .					
	17 Compensation of officers, directors, and trustees (attach schedule)					
	18 Other salaries and wages . .					
	19 Interest					
	20 Occupancy (rent, utilities, etc.) .					
	21 Depreciation and depletion . .					
	22 Other (attach schedule) . . .					
	23 **Total** expenses (add lines 14 through 22)					
	24 Excess of revenue over expenses (line 13 minus line 23)					

Part IV   **Financial Data** *(Continued)*

B. Balance Sheet (at the end of the period shown)		Current tax year Date ....
Assets		
1	Cash	**1**	
2	Accounts receivable, net	**2**	
3	Inventories	**3**	
4	Bonds and notes receivable (attach schedule)	**4**	
5	Corporate stocks (attach schedule).	**5**	
6	Mortgage loans (attach schedule)	**6**	
7	Other investments (attach schedule)	**7**	
8	Depreciable and depletable assets (attach schedule)	**8**	
9	Land	**9**	
10	Other assets (attach schedule)	**10**	
11	**Total assets** (add lines 1 through 10)	**11**	
Liabilities		
12	Accounts payable	**12**	
13	Contributions, gifts, grants, etc., payable	**13**	
14	Mortgages and notes payable (attach schedule)	**14**	
15	Other liabilities (attach schedule)	**15**	
16	**Total liabilities** (add lines 12 through 15)	**16**	
Fund Balances or Net Assets		
17	Total fund balances or net assets	**17**	
18	**Total liabilities and fund balances or net assets** (add line 16 and line 17)	**18**	

If there has been any substantial change in any aspect of the organization's financial activities since the end of the period shown above, check the box and attach a detailed explanation . . . . ▶ ☐

Application for Exemption From Self-Employment Tax for Use by Ministers, Members of Religious Orders and Christian Science Practitioners

OMB No. 1545-0168
Expires 6-30-94

File Original and Two Copies

File original and two copies and attach supporting documents. This exemption is granted only if the IRS returns a copy to you marked "approved."

Please type or print

1 Name of taxpayer shown on Form 1040	Social security number
Number and street (including apt. no.)	Telephone number (optional) ( )
City or town, state, and ZIP code	

2 Check ONE box: ☐ Christian Science practitioner   ☐ Ordained minister, priest, rabbi
☐ Member of religious order not under a vow of poverty   ☐ Commissioned or licensed minister (see line 6)

3 Date ordained, licensed, etc. (Attach supporting document. See instructions.)
/   /

4 Legal name of ordaining, licensing, or commissioning body or religious order

Number, street, and room or suite no.

Employer identification number

City or town, state, and ZIP code

5 Enter the first 2 years, after the date shown on line 3, that you had net self-employment earnings of $400 or more, any of which came from services as a minister, priest, rabbi, etc.; member of a religious order; or Christian Science practitioner ▶   19 __   19 __

6 If you apply for the exemption as a licensed or commissioned minister, and your denomination also ordains ministers, please indicate how your ecclesiastical powers differ from those of an ordained minister of your denomination. Attach a copy of your denomination's by-laws relating to the powers of ordained, commissioned, or licensed ministers.

---

7 I certify that I am conscientiously opposed to, or because of my religious principles I am opposed to, the acceptance (for services I perform as a minister, member of a religious order not under a vow of poverty, or a Christian Science practitioner) of any public insurance that makes payments in the event of death, disability, old age, or retirement; or that makes payments toward the cost of, or provides services for, medical care. (Public insurance includes insurance systems established by the Social Security Act.)

I certify that as a duly ordained, commissioned, or licensed minister of a church or a member of a religious order not under a vow of poverty, I have informed the ordaining, commissioning, or licensing body of my church or order that I am conscientiously opposed to, or because of religious principles, I am opposed to the acceptance (for services I perform as a minister or as a member of a religious order) of any public insurance that makes payments in the event of death, disability, old age, or retirement; or that makes payments toward the cost of, or provides services for, medical care, including the benefits of any insurance system established by the Social Security Act.

I certify that I did not file an effective waiver certificate (Form 2031) electing social security coverage on earnings as a minister, member of a religious order not under a vow of poverty, or a Christian Science practitioner.

I request to be exempted from paying self-employment tax on my earnings from services as a minister, member of a religious order under a vow of poverty, or a Christian Science practitioner, under section 1402(e) of the Internal Revenue Code. I understand that the exemption, if granted, will apply only to these earnings. Under penalties of perjury, I declare that I have examined this application and to the best of my knowledge and belief, it is true and correct.

Signature ▶   Date ▶

Caution: Form 4361 is **not proof** of the right to an exemption from Federal income tax withholding or social security tax, the right to a parsonage allowance exclusion (section 107), assignment by your religious superiors to a particular job, or the exemption or church status of the ordaining, licensing, commissioning body, or religious order.

For Internal Revenue Service Use

☐ Approved for exemption from self-employment tax on ministerial earnings
☐ Disapproved for exemption from self-employment tax on ministerial earnings

By ....
(Director's signature)   (Date)

General Instructions

(Section references are to the Internal Revenue Code.)

Paperwork Reduction Act Notice.—We ask for the information on this form to carry out the Internal Revenue laws of the United States. You are required to give us the information. We need it to ensure that you are complying with these laws and to allow us to figure and collect the right amount of tax.

The time needed to complete and file this form will vary depending on individual circumstances. The estimated average time is:

Recordkeeping, 7 minutes; Learning about the law or the form, 19 minutes; Preparing the form, 16 minutes; Copying, assembling, and sending the form to IRS, 17 minutes.

If you have comments concerning the accuracy of these time estimates or

suggestions for making this form more simple, we would be happy to hear from you. You can write to both the **Internal Revenue Service**, Washington, DC 20224, Attention: IRS Reports Clearance Officer, T:FP; and the **Office of Management and Budget**, Paperwork Reduction Project (1545-0168), Washington, DC 20503. **DO NOT** send the form to either of these offices. Instead, see **Where To File** on page 2.

Purpose of Form.—File Form 4361 to apply for an exemption from self-employment tax if you are:

● An ordained, commissioned, or licensed minister of a church;

● A member of a religious order who has not taken a vow of poverty;

● A Christian Science practitioner; or

● A commissioned or licensed minister of a church or church denomination that

ordains ministers, if you have authority to perform substantially all religious duties of your church or denomination.

This application must be based on your religious or conscientious opposition to the acceptance (for services performed as a minister, member of a religious order, or Christian Science practitioner) of any public insurance that makes payments for death, disability, old age, or retirement; or that makes payments for the cost of, or provides services for, medical care, including any insurance benefits established by the Social Security Act.

If you are a duly ordained, commissioned, or licensed minister of a church or a member of a religious order not under a vow of poverty, prior to filing this form you must inform the ordaining, commissioning, or

(continued on page 2)

Cat. No. 41586H

Form **4361** (Rev. 6-91)

licensing body of your church or order that you are opposed to the acceptance of public insurance benefits based on ministerial service on religious or conscientious grounds.

Do not file Form 4361 if:

● You ever filed a waiver certificate (Form 2031); or

● You belong to a religious order and took a vow of poverty. You are automatically exempt from self-employment tax on earnings for services you perform for your church or its agencies. No tax exemption applies to earnings for services you perform for any other organization.

Additional Information.—For more information, get **Pub. 517,** Social Security for Members of the Clergy and Religious Workers.

When To File.—File Form 4361 by the date your tax return is due, including extensions, for the second tax year in which you had at least $400 of net earnings from self-employment, any of which came from services performed as a minister, member of a religious order, or Christian Science practitioner.

Effective Date of Exemption.—An exemption from self-employment tax is effective for all tax years ending after 1967 in which you have net self-employment earnings of $400 or more, if you derive any of it from ministerial services. For example, if you had qualified net earnings of $400 or more in 1968 and not again until 1991, a valid Form 4361 filed by April 15, 1992, would apply to 1968 and all later years. Refer to Pub. 517 to see if you are entitled to a refund of self-employment tax paid in earlier years.

Where To File.—Mail the original and two copies of this form to the **Internal Revenue Service Center** for the place where you live.

If you live in:	Use this address:
Florida, Georgia, South Carolina	Atlanta, GA 39901
New Jersey, New York City and counties of Nassau, Rockland, Suffolk, and Westchester	Holtsville, NY 00501
Connecticut, Maine, Massachusetts, New Hampshire, New York (all other counties), Rhode Island, Vermont	Andover, MA 05501
Delaware, District of Columbia, Maryland, Pennsylvania, Virginia	Philadelphia, PA 19255
Illinois, Iowa, Minnesota, Missouri, Wisconsin	Kansas City, MO 64999
Indiana, Kentucky, Michigan, Ohio, West Virginia	Cincinnati, OH 45999
Kansas, New Mexico, Oklahoma, Texas	Austin, TX 73301
Alaska, Arizona, California (counties of Alpine, Amador, Butte, Calaveras, Colusa, Contra Costa, Del Norte, El Dorado, Glenn, Humboldt, Lake, Lassen, Marin, Mendocino, Modoc, Napa, Nevada, Placer, Plumas, Sacramento, San Joaquin, Shasta, Sierra, Siskiyou, Solano, Sonoma, Sutter, Tehama, Trinity, Yolo, and Yuba), Colorado, Idaho, Montana, Nebraska, Nevada, North Dakota, Oregon, South Dakota, Utah, Washington, Wyoming	Ogden, UT 84201
California (all other counties), Hawaii	Fresno, CA 93888
Alabama, Arkansas, Louisiana, Mississippi, North Carolina, Tennessee	Memphis, TN 37501

American Samoa	Philadelphia, PA 19255
Guam	Commissioner of Revenue and Taxation 855 West Marine Drive Agana, GU 96910
Northern Mariana Islands (Commonwealth of the)	Philadelphia, PA 19255
Puerto Rico (or if excluding income under section 933) Virgin Islands: Nonpermanent residents	Philadelphia, PA 19255
Virgin Islands: Permanent residents	V.I. Bureau of Internal Revenue Lockharts Garden No. 1A Charlotte Amalie St. Thomas, VI 00802
Foreign country: U.S. citizens and those filing Form 2555 or Form 4563	Philadelphia, PA 19255
All A.P.O. or F.P.O. addresses	Philadelphia, PA 19255

Approval of Application.— Before your application can be approved, the IRS must verify that you are aware of the grounds for exemption and that you want the exemption on that basis. When your completed Form 4361 is received, the IRS will mail you a statement that describes the grounds for receiving an exemption under section 1402(e). You must certify that you have read the statement and seek exemption on the grounds listed on the statement. The certification must be made by signing a copy of the statement under penalties of perjury and mailing it to the IRS service center that issued it, not later than 90 days after the date the statement was mailed to you. If it is not mailed by that time, your exemption will not be effective until the date the signed copy is received by the service center.

If your application is approved, a copy of Form 4361 will be returned to you marked "approved." Once the exemption is approved, you cannot revoke it.

Earnings To Which Exemption Applies.— Only earnings from ministerial services are exempt from self-employment tax.

Conducting religious worship services or ministering sacerdotal functions are ministerial services whether or not performed for a religious organization.

Ministerial services also include those performed under the authority of a church or church denomination. Examples are controlling, conducting, and maintaining religious organizations, including religious boards, societies, and other agencies integral to these organizations.

If your church assigns or designates you to perform services for an organization that is neither a religious organization nor an integral agency of a religious organization, you are performing ministerial services, even though they may not involve conducting religious worship or ministering sacerdotal functions. Your services are ordinarily not considered assigned or designated by your church if any of the following is true:

● The organization for which you perform the services did not arrange with your church for your services.

● You perform the same services for the organization as other employees not designated as you were.

● You perform the same services before and after the designation.

Earnings To Which Exemption Does Not Apply.—Exemption from self-employment tax does not apply to earnings from services that are not ministerial.

Earnings from the following entities are not exempt even if religious services are conducted or sacerdotal functions are ministered: the United States; a state, territory, or possession of the U.S.; the District of Columbia; a foreign government; or a subdivision of any of these bodies. For example, chaplains in the U.S. Armed Forces are considered commissioned officers, not ministers. Similarly, chaplains in state prisons or universities are considered civil servants.

Indicating Exemption on Form 1040.—If the IRS returned your application marked "approved" and your only self-employment income was from ministerial services, write "Exempt—Form 4361" on the self-employment line in the **Other Taxes** section of Form 1040. If you had other self-employment income, see **Schedule SE** (Form 1040).

Specific Instructions

Line 1—Social Security Number.—Enter your social security number. If you do not have one, file **Form SS-5,** Application for a Social Security Card, with your local Social Security Administration office. If you do not receive your card in time, file Form 4361 and enter "applied for" in the space for your social security number.

Line 3.—Enter the date you were ordained, commissioned, or licensed as a minister of a church; became a member of a religious order; or began practice as a Christian Science practitioner. Do not file Form 4361 before this date. Attach a copy of the certificate (or, if you did not receive one, a letter from the governing body of your church) that establishes your status as an ordained, commissioned, or licensed minister; a member of a religious order; or a Christian Science practitioner.

Line 4.—If you are a minister or belong to a religious order, enter the legal name, address, and employer identification number of the denomination that ordained, commissioned, or licensed you, or the order to which you belong. Get the employer identification number from your church or order.

You must be able to show that the body that ordained, commissioned, or licensed you, or your religious order, is exempt from Federal income tax under section 501(a) as a religious organization described in section 501(c)(3). You must also be able to show that the body is a church (or convention or association of churches) described in section 170(b)(1)(A)(i). To assist the service center in processing your application, you can attach a copy of the exemption letter issued to the organization by the IRS. If that is not available, you can attach a letter signed by an individual authorized to act for the organization stating that the organization meets both of the above requirements.

*U.S. Government Printing Office: 1991 — 299-982/49197

SCHEDULE SE	Self-Employment Tax	OMB No. 1545-0074

SCHEDULE SE

(Form 1040)

Department of the Treasury
Internal Revenue Service   (O)

Self-Employment Tax

▶ See Instructions for Schedule SE (Form 1040).

▶ **Attach to Form 1040.**

OMB No. 1545-0074

1993

Attachment
Sequence No. **17**

Name of person with **self-employment** income (as shown on Form 1040)	Social security number of person with **self-employment** income ▶	

Who Must File Schedule SE

You must file Schedule SE if:

- Your wages (and tips) subject to social security AND Medicare tax (or railroad retirement tax) were less than $135,000; **AND**
- Your net earnings from self-employment from other than church employee income (line 4 of Short Schedule SE or line 4c of Long Schedule SE) were $400 or more; **OR**
- You had church employee income of $108.28 or more. Income from services you performed as a minister or a member of a religious order **is not** church employee income. See page SE-1.

Note: *Even if you have a loss or a small amount of income from self-employment, it may be to your benefit to file Schedule SE and use either "optional method" in Part II of Long Schedule SE. See page SE-3.*

Exception. If your only self-employment income was from earnings as a minister, member of a religious order, or Christian Science practitioner, **AND** you filed Form 4361 and received IRS approval not to be taxed on those earnings, **DO NOT** file Schedule SE. Instead, write "Exempt–Form 4361" on Form 1040, line 47.

May I Use Short Schedule SE or MUST I Use Long Schedule SE?

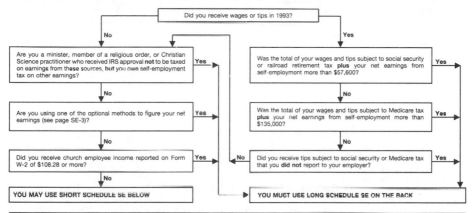

Section A—Short Schedule SE. Caution: *Read above to see if you can use Short Schedule SE.*

1	Net farm profit or (loss) from Schedule F, line 36, and farm partnerships, Schedule K-1 (Form 1065), line 15a	1	
2	Net profit or (loss) from Schedule C, line 31; Schedule C-EZ, line 3; and Schedule K-1 (Form 1065), line 15a (other than farming). Ministers and members of religious orders see page SE-1 for amounts to report on this line. See page SE-2 for other income to report	2	
3	Combine lines 1 and 2	3	
4	**Net earnings from self-employment.** Multiply line 3 by 92.35% (.9235). If less than $400, **do not** file this schedule; you do not owe self-employment tax . . . . ▶	4	
5	**Self-employment tax.** If the amount on line 4 is: • $57,600 or less, multiply line 4 by 15.3% (.153) and enter the result. • More than $57,600 but less than $135,000, multiply the amount in excess of $57,600 by 2.9% (.029). Then, add $8,812.80 to the result and enter the total. • $135,000 or more, enter $11,057.40. Also enter on **Form 1040, line 47. (Important:** You are allowed a deduction for **one-half** of this amount. Multiply line 5 by 50% (.5) and enter the result on **Form 1040, line 25.)**	5	

For Paperwork Reduction Act Notice, see Form 1040 instructions.   Cat. No. 11358Z   Schedule SE (Form 1040) 1993

Name of person with **self-employment** income (as shown on Form 1040)	Social security number of person with **self-employment** income ▶		

Section B—Long Schedule SE

Part I   Self-Employment Tax

Note: *If your only income subject to self-employment tax is church employee income, skip lines 1 through 4b. Enter -0- on line 4c and go to line 5a. Income from services you performed as a minister or a member of a religious order is not church employee income. See page SE-1.*

A   If you are a minister, member of a religious order, or Christian Science practitioner **AND** you filed Form 4361, but you had $400 or more of **other** net earnings from self-employment, check here and continue with Part I . . . . . . ▶ ☐

1	Net farm profit or (loss) from Schedule F, line 36, and farm partnerships, Schedule K-1 (Form 1065), line 15a. **Note:** *Skip this line if you use the farm optional method. See page SE-3* . .	**1**	
2	Net profit or (loss) from Schedule C, line 31; Schedule C-EZ, line 3; and Schedule K-1 (Form 1065), line 15a (other than farming). Ministers and members of religious orders see page SE-1 for amounts to report on this line. See page SE-2 for other income to report. **Note:** *Skip this line if you use the nonfarm optional method. See page SE-3*	**2**	
3	Combine lines 1 and 2	**3**	
4a	If line 3 is more than zero, multiply line 3 by 92.35% (.9235). Otherwise, enter amount from line 3	**4a**	
b	If you elected one or both of the optional methods, enter the total of lines 17 and 19 here . .	**4b**	
c	Combine lines 4a and 4b. If less than $400, **do not** file this schedule; you do not owe self-employment tax. **Exception.** If less than $400 and you had church employee income, enter -0- and continue . ▶	**4c**	
5a	Enter your church employee income from Form W-2. **Caution:** *See page SE-1 for definition of church employee income* **5a**	**5b**	
b	Multiply line 5a by 92.35% (.9235). If less than $100, enter -0-	**5b**	
6	**Net earnings from self-employment.** Add lines 4c and 5b	**6**	
7	Maximum amount of combined wages and self-employment earnings subject to social security tax or the 6.2% portion of the 7.65% railroad retirement (tier 1) tax for 1993	**7**	57,600 00
8a	Total social security wages and tips (from Form(s) W-2) and railroad retirement (tier 1) compensation **8a**		
b	Unreported tips subject to social security tax (from Form 4137, line 9) **8b**		
c	Add lines 8a and 8b	**8c**	
9	Subtract line 8c from line 7. If zero or less, enter -0- here and on line 10 and go to line 12a ▶	**9**	
10	Multiply the **smaller** of line 6 or line 9 by 12.4% (.124)	**10**	
11	Maximum amount of combined wages and self-employment earnings subject to Medicare tax or the 1.45% portion of the 7.65% railroad retirement (tier 1) tax for 1993	**11**	135,000 00
12a	Total Medicare wages and tips (from Form(s) W-2) and railroad retirement (tier 1) compensation **12a**		
b	Unreported tips subject to Medicare tax (from Form 4137, line 14) . **12b**		
c	Add lines 12a and 12b	**12c**	
13	Subtract line 12c from line 11. If zero or less, enter -0- here and on line 14 and go to line 15 .	**13**	
14	Multiply the **smaller** of line 6 or line 13 by 2.9% (.029) . . . . . /.	**14**	
15	**Self-employment tax.** Add lines 10 and 14. Enter here and on **Form 1040, line 47. (Important:** You are allowed a deduction for **one-half** of this amount. Multiply line 15 by 50% (.5) and enter the result on **Form 1040, line 25.)**	**15**	

Part II   Optional Methods To Figure Net Earnings (See page SE-3.)

Farm Optional Method. You may use this method **only** if **(a)** Your gross farm income[1] was not more than $2,400 **or (b)** Your gross farm income[1] was more than $2,400 and your net farm profits[2] were less than $1,733.

16	Maximum income for optional methods	**16**	1,600 00
17	Enter the **smaller** of: two-thirds (⅔) of gross farm income[1] (not less than zero) **or** $1,600. Also, include this amount on line 4b above	**17**	

Nonfarm Optional Method. You may use this method **only** if **(a)** Your net nonfarm profits[3] were less than $1,733 and also less than 72.189% of your gross nonfarm income,[4] **and (b)** You had net earnings from self-employment of at least $400 in 2 of the prior 3 years. **Caution:** *You may use this method no more than five times.*

18	Subtract line 17 from line 16	**18**	
19	Enter the **smaller** of: two-thirds (⅔) of gross nonfarm income[4] (not less than zero) **or** the amount on line 18. Also, include this amount on line 4b above	**19**	

[1]From Schedule F, line 11, and Schedule K-1 (Form 1065), line 15b.   [3]From Schedule C, line 31; Schedule C-EZ, line 3; and Schedule K-1 (Form 1065), line 15a.
[2]From Schedule F, line 36, and Schedule K-1 (Form 1065), line 15a.   [4]From Schedule C, line 7; Schedule C-EZ, line 1; and Schedule K-1 (Form 1065), line 15c.

PRODUCER/ARTIST AGREEMENT

AGREEMENT made and entered into as of this ____ day of _____, 1993 by and between parties, GREATER CHRIST PUBLISHING ("Producer"), and PETER PAUL known herein as ("Artist").

WITNESSETH:

1. For purposes of this agreement.

DEFINITION

(a) "Side" means the equivalent of a 7-inch, 45 rpm single-sided recording embodying the recorded performances of the Artist and intended to use in the manufacture and sale of phonograph records.

(b) "Single" means a 7-inch, 45 rpm double-sided phonograph record embodying thereon two (2) Sides.

(c) "LP" means a 12-inch, 33-1/3 rpm double-sided phonograph record embodying thereon the equivalent of not less than seven (7) Sides and not more than twelve (12) Sides.

(d) "Records", "phonograph records" "recordings", and "derivatives" means and includes all forms of recording and reproductions, now known or which may hereafter become known, manufactured or sold primarily for home use and/or juke box use and/or use on or in means of transportation, including, without limiting the generality of the foregoing, magnetic recording tape, film, electronic video recordings and any other medium or device of the reproduction of artistic performances or sold primarily for home and/or juke box use, and/or on or in means of transportation, whether embodying:

   (i) Sound alone, or

   (ii) Sound synchronized with visual images, e.g. "sight and sound" devices.

(e) "Suggested Retail List Price"("SRLP") means the applicable retail list price in the country of manufacture (exclusive of all taxes, discounts, duties and packaging); which SRLP is currently $8.98 in the United States.

(f) "Composition" means a musical composition or medley consisting of words and/or music, embodied in a side.

(g) "Union Scale" means the applicable minimum payments required to be made to Artist under the applicable collective bargaining agreement as may be in force from time to time and controlling with respect to this agreement.

If, at any time, there is no such collective bargaining agreement in force, then union scale shall mean the union scale in the collective bargaining agreement last in effect.

(h) "Recording Costs" means all costs incurred for and with respect to the production of Sides embodying Artist's performances. Recording Costs include, without limitation to, union scale, the costs of all instruments, musicians, vocalists, conductors, arrangers, orchestrators, copyists, etc., payments to a trustee or fund based on wages to the extent required by an agreement between Producer and any labor organization or trustee, all studio costs, tape, editing, mixing, engineering, travel and perdiems for individuals involved in production of the Sides, rehearsal halls, costs of non-studio facilities and equipment, dubbing, transportation of instruments, producer's fees and other costs, and expenses incurred in producing the Sides hereunder, from time to time, and which are customarily recognized as Recording Costs in the phonograph record industry.

(i) "Territory" means the world.

(j) "Distribution Company" means the third-party record company which distributes Producer's phonograph records embodying Artist's performances.

2. Producer hereby engages Artist to render such services as it may require in the production of phonograph records and Artist hereby accepts such engagement and agrees to render such services exclusively to Producer for an initial recording term period of one (1) year commencing on the date hereof and additional period or periods, if any, by which such initial period may be extended through Producer's exercise of one or more of the options granted to Producer herein. The initial period as same may be extended is hereinafter called the "Term." Artist hereby irrevocably grants to Producer the option to extend the initial period of one (1) year (through three (3) consecutive renewal periods of one (1) year each) if Producer has fulfilled his obligations herein and has obtained a recording contract for Artist. Unless Producer shall notify Artist at least thirty (30) days prior to the date the Term would otherwise expire, it shall be deemed to have exercised the next succeeding option. Each year of the Term shall hereinafter be referred to as a "Contract Year."

3. (a) During the Term Artist agrees to perform for the recording of Sides, embodying Compositions not heretofore recorded by Artist, in recording studios selected by Producer and each recording session. The Compositions to be recorded shall be designated by Producer and each recording shall be subject to Producer's approval as satisfactory for the manufacture and sale of phonograph records. Upon the request of Producer, Artist shall rerecord any Composition until a satisfactory master record shall have been obtained. Should Artist fail to appear at any recording session of which Artist has been given reasonable notice, for any reason, Producer shall have the right to charge any of its out-of-pocket expenses in respect of such session against Artist's royalties if and when earned.

   (b) During each Contract Year, Producer shall request and Artist shall perform for the recording on one (1) LP. It is agreed that the foregoing is a minimum and that during each Contract Year Producer may request, and upon such request Artist shall perform for, the recording of such number of additional Sides as Company may request, but not more than shall be sufficient for two (2) additional LP's. If the Producer fails to request and assist with the recording of the album this Contract shall be void.

4. All sides recorded during the Term and all derivatives manufactured therefrom, together with the performances embodied thereon shall from the inception of their creation be entirely and forever the property of Producer and/or the distribution company, free from any claims whatsoever by artist or any person, firm or corporation deriving any rights or interests from Artist; and Producer and/or the distribution company shall have the right to copyright the Sides in Producer's and/or the distribution company's name as the owner and author thereof and to secure any and all renewals of such copyright. Without limiting the generality of the foregoing, Producer and/or the distribution company and/or their subsidiaries, affiliates, and licensees, shall have the exclusive and unlimited right to all the products of the services of Artist hereunder, including but not limited to, the exclusive and unlimited right throughout the world.

   (a) To manufacture, produce, advertise, publicize, sell, distribute, lease, license, or otherwise use or dispose of the Sides and phonograph records and other reproductions embodying the Sides in any or all fields of use, by any method now or hereafter known, upon such terms and conditions as Producer and/or the distribution company may elect or, in their sole discretion, to refrain from them.

(b) To use and publish and to permit others to use and publish the name, professional name, photograph and likeness of Artist, and biographical material concerning the Artist, for advertising, purposes of trade and otherwise without restriction, in connection with the phonograph records made pursuant hereto; exception of merchandizing rights reserved to Artist.

(c) To release derivatives of any one or more of the Sides on any medium or device now or hereafter known, under any name, trademark or label which Producer and/or the distribution company, their subsidiaries, affiliates and licensees may from time to time elect;

(d) To perform the Sides publicly and to permit the public performance thereof by means of radio broadcast, television and/or by any method now or hereafter known; and

(e) To incorporate without cost to Producer from time to time in phonograph records to be made hereunder instrumentations, orchestrations and arrangements owned by Artist of Compositions to be recorded hereunder.

5. (a) During the Term, Artist agrees not to perform, or to license or consent to the use of Artist's name, likeness, voice, biographical material or other identification (hereinafter called "Artist's Identification"), for or in connection with the recording or exploitation of phonograph records, by or for anyone other than Producer.

(b) Artist further agrees not to perform, or to license or consent to the use by any one or more third parties, of Artist's Identification, for or in connection with the recording or exploitation of any phonograph record embodying any Composition recorded by Artist under this agreement prior to the latter of:

(i) Two (2) years after the period or renewal exercised by the producer subsequent to the date such Composition is recorded hereunder. Should Artist so perform or should a licensed or consented use of Artist's Identification by any one or more third parties occur in connection with any such Composition during the period referred to above, then in addition to any of Producer's other rights or remedies, Producer shall have no further obligation to pay future royalties to Artist which otherwise would accrue to

Artist hereunder for sales of records which contain Artist's performance of such Composition.

6. Producer shall pay to Artist the following royalties for the sale by Producer, the distribution company or their licensees of phonograph records derived from the Sides against which all sums advanced to or on behalf of Artist, including, but not limited to, those referred to in Paragraph 8, shall be chargeable and from which Producer shall recoup such sums:

    (a) Conditioned upon your full and faithful performance of all the terms and conditions hereof, you will be paid royalties on Net Sales of records as hereinafter set forth:
    Company will pay you as a basic property, the percentage set forth in the following schedule, of the applicable Royalties Base Price in respect of ninety (90%) percent of Net Sales of Phonograph Records in disc form, consisting entirely of Master Recordings performed by you and recorded hereunder and sold by Company or its Licensees through normal retail channels for distribution in the United States of America.

    (b) During each Contract Year, you shall render your services to Company in accordance with the terms and conditions hereof in connection with recording the minimum number of Sides (the "Minimum Recording Commitment") set forth in the following schedule:

CONTRACT YEAR	BASIC ROYALTY	MINIMUM RECORDING COMMITMENT
FIRST	6%	LP Equivalent
SECOND	6.25%	8 Sides or LP Equivalent
THIRD	6.75%	8 Sides or LP Equivalent
FOURTH	7.00%	8 Sides or LP Equivalent

Company shall have the right to increase your recording commitment in respect of any Contract Year, and you shall render to Company your exclusive services as a recording Artist in connection with such additional number of Sides in excess of the Minimum Recording Commitment as Company may request, from time to time. When Artist record sales are as follows, enumeration of bonus shall be paid to artist as:

UNIT SALES	UNITS SOLD
500,000	6.25%
1,000,000	6.50%

(c) A basic royalty of six (6%) percent of ninety percent (90%) SRLP, for all phonograph records derived from the Sides, manufactured and sold by Producer and/or the distribution company for distribution in the United States, paid for and not returned.

(d) A royalty equal to one half of royalty rate set forth in subparagraph (a) above, for all phonograph records derived from the Sides, manufactured and sold for distribution outside of the United States by Producer, the distribution company, or their licensees, paid for and not returned.

(e) Royalties for phonograph records sold outside the United States shall be computed in the national currency of the country of manufacture or the country to sale as Producer is paid, and shall be paid at the same rate of exchange as Producer is paid, provided, however, that royalties on phonograph records sold outside the United States shall not be due and payable by Producer until payment heretofore has been received by Producer in the United States, in the United States Dollars and provided further, that if Producer shall not receive payment in the United States, in United States Dollars, Producer shall elect to accept payment in a foreign country and in foreign currency.

Producer may deposit to the credit of Artist (and at the expense of Artist) in such country in a depository selected by Producer, payments so received applicable to royalties hereunder, and shall notify Artist promptly thereof. Deposit as aforesaid shall fulfill the obligations of Producer as to phonograph record sales to which such royalty payments are applicable.

(f) As to records not consisting entirely of the Sides, Artist's royalties otherwise payable hereunder shall be prorated on the basis of the number of such Sides which are on such records compared to the total number of recordings on such records.

(g) Royalties on phonograph records included in albums, jackets, boxes, or any other type of package or container (herein collectively referred to as "containers") shall be based solely upon the retail list price of such phonograph records in containers less all taxes and also less the container charge which is charged by the distribution company.

(h) For records sold to distributors or others for less than the regular wholesale price or at a discount therefrom, but for more than fifty (50%) percent of the regular wholesale price, the rate of royalty payable by the Producer to Artist as above provided, shall be reduced in the same proportion as the reduction in the regular wholesale price.

(i) For long playing records, discs, or tapes (other than promotional records hereinafter provided for) sold as budget records, the royalty rate shall be one-half (1/2) of the otherwise applicable royalty rate.

(j) For records sold through record clubs or similar sales plans or devices, the royalty rate shall be one-half (1/2) of the royalty rate otherwise applicable, royalties shall be accounted for on the same basis as Producer is accounted to by its licensee and no royalty shall be payable with respect to records distributed to members of record clubs as "bonus " or "free " records, as a result of joining the club, and/or recommending that another join the club, and/or purchasing a required number of records.

(k) In computing the number of records sold hereunder, Producer shall have the right to deduct Returns and Credits or add in of any nature, including, without limitation, (i) those on account of any return or exchange privilege, (ii) defective merchandise, and (iii) error in billing or shipment.

Producer shall have the right to withhold a reasonable portion of Artist's royalties as a reserve in accordance with the standard accounting practice and procedures of the distribution company.

(l) Producer and/or the distribution company shall have the right to sell records under any merchandising plans or terms it may deem desirable. No royalty shall be payable for records returned for credit by any buyer, for records given away or sold for fifty (50%) percent or less of the regular wholesale price, for records used for the purpose of publicity or advertising, for records distributed to disc jockeys, radio stations, television stations, motion picture companies, publishers, or others, for records used on transportation facilities, for records sold as cut-outs, or for records sold as scrap.

(m) Producer and/or the distribution company shall have the right to include or to license others to include any one or more of the Sides in promotional records on which such Sides and other recordings are included, which promotional records are designed for sale at a substantially lower price than the regular price of Company's long play records, but not more than two (2) of the Sides shall be included in any one such promotional record. No royalties shall be payable on sales of such promotional records.

(n) The royalty rate payable hereunder for records sold as premiums shall be one-half (1/2) the royalty rate otherwise applicable and the retail list price for such records shall be deemed to be Producer's or the distribution company's actual sales price. Producer and/or the distribution company shall be entitled to use and publish, and to license or permit others to use and publish, Artist's Identification with respect to the products or services in connection with which such "premium " records are sold or distributed but not as an endorsement of any product or service.

(o) Producer and/or the distribution company shall have the right to license the Sides to third parties for phonograph record use and all other types of use on a flat-fee basis. Producer shall credit Artist's royalty account with twenty-five (25%) percent of the amount received by Producer under such license.

(p) For sales of records which include Sides subject hereto which are sold through the method known as "key outlet marketing" by distribution through retail fulfillment centers in conjunction with special advertisements on radio or television, the method known as direct mail or mail order, or by any combination of the methods set forth above, Producer shall credit Artist's royalty account with a sum equal to fifty (50%) percent of the net royalty receipts received by Producer from such sales.

(q) The royalty rate for records sold for sale in Armed Forces Post Exchanges shall be one-half (1/2) the applicable royalty rate provided for in sub-paragraph (a) above.

(r) With respect to any Side embodying Artist's performance hereunder together with the performance of another artist or artists to whom Producer is obligated to pay royalties in respect of phonograph records embodying the joint performances contained in such Side: (i) the royalty rate to be used in determining the royalties payable to Artist in respect of such Side shall be computed by multiplying the royalty rate otherwise applicable thereto by a fraction, the numerator of which shall be one and the denominator of which shall be the total number of royalty artists whose performances are embodied on such Side, and (ii) in determining the portion of Recording Costs applicable to such Side which shall be charged against Artist's royalties, if any when earned, such proportion shall be computed by multiplying the aggregated amount of such Recording Costs by the same fraction used in determining the royalties payable to Artist in respect to Such Side. It is specifically understood and agreed, however, that Artist shall not be required to perform hereunder together with any such other artist or artist unless Artist shall have consented thereto, and that no such joint recording shall be counted toward the fulfillment of Artist's minimum recording obligation hereunder unless Producer consents, in writing to such joint recording; then it will be deemed toward the fulfillment of Artist's recording obligation.

(s) If Producer causes records manufactured from the Sides recorded pursuant to this agreement to be distributed by a third party record company, the royalties due and payable to Artist shall be computed upon the same basis as that upon which Producer is paid by such third party record company. Similarly, the label restriction, coupling and other sales restrictions, free goods limitations and requirements with respect to specificity of accounting, to which Producer is entitled in its agreement with such third party record company, shall be deemed to inure to Artist's benefit as well as to Producer's.

7. Accounting as to royalties payable hereunder shall be made by Producer to Artist together with payment of accrued royalties, if any, earned by Artist during the preceding half-year. All royalty statements rendered by Producer to Artist shall be binding upon Artist and not subject to any objection by Artist for any reason unless specific objections in writing, stating the basis thereof, is given to Producer within one (1) year from the date rendered. Artist shall have the right to appoint a certified public accountant or attorney to inspect the books and records of Producer insofar as the same pertain to the subject matter of this agreement, provided, however, that such inspection shall take place only upon reasonable notice, not more frequently than once in any calendar year unless there is grave error during which Artist receives a statement, and at the sole expense of Artist.

8. Producer shall specify and shall advance all Recording Costs incurred in connection with the production of Sides requested by Producer hereunder, which sums shall be recoupable by Producer from royalties due Artist hereunder.

9. During the Term, Artist will from time to time, at Producer and/or the distribution company's request and expense, whenever the

same will not unreasonably interfere with other professional activities of Artist, appear for photography, poster, and cover art, etc., under the direction of the Producer, the distribution company, or their nominees and will appear for interviews with representatives of the communications media and Producer's and/or the distribution company's publicity personnel and will perform other reasonable promotional services.

10. The Artist expressly agrees that Artist's services hereunder are of a special and unique character, and that in the event of a breach by Artist of any term, condition, or covenant herein, Producer shall be entitled to seek injunctive relief in addition to any other remedies available to it.

11. Artist warrants and represents that:

    (a) There are now in existence no prior recorded performances by Artist unreleased within the United States, except those set forth on Schedule "A" annexed hereto and made a part hereof.

    (b) There are not now and during the Term shall not be any restrictions with respect to compositions Artist is legally able to perform for Producer hereunder, except those set forth on Schedule "B " annexed hereto and made a part hereof.

    (c) Artist is not now and during the Term shall not be a party to or bound by any contract or agreement of any kind which will interfere in any manner with complete performance of the within agreement by Artist. Artist is under no disability, restriction, or prohibition with respect to Artist's right to sign and perform under this agreement.

    (d) The performances embodied in the Sides do not and will not infringe upon the rights of any person or business entity.

    (e) Artist has the right to use Artist's name and professional name and grants to Producer and the distribution company during the Term the exclusive right to use and to allow others to use said names and any professional name adopted by Artist for phonograph record purposes and the exclusive right to such use thereafter in connection with the recordings subject hereto. Producer's use of such names in accordance with the terms hereof will not infringe upon the rights of any third party.

    (f) Artist agrees to and does hereby indemnify, save, and hold Producer harmless of and from any and all loss and damage (including reasonable attorney's fee) arising out of or connected with any claim by any one or more third parties which is inconsistent with any of the warranties, representations, and/or agreements made by Artist herein, and agrees to reimburse Producer on demand for any payment made by it at any time with respect to any liability or claim to which the foregoing indemnity applies.

12. (a) Producer reserves the right to extend the Term for the duration of the following contingencies, if, by reason of such contingencies, it is materially hampered in the recording, manufacture, distribution, or sale of records, or its normal business operations becomes commercially impracticable by labor disagreements, fire, catastrophe, shortage of materials, or any cause beyond Producer's control. A number of days equal to the total of all such days of extension shall be added to the Contract Year in which such contingency shall occur and the time for Producer to mail written notice to Artist pursuant to Paragraph 2 and the date of commencement of subsequent Contract Years shall be deemed extended accordingly.

(b) In the event of any default or breach by Artist in the performance of any of Artist's obligations hereunder, Producer, in addition to any other rights or remedies which it may have at law or otherwise, may terminate the Term or may suspend its obligations hereunder for the duration of such default or breach and until the same has been cured, and may at its election extend the Term for a period equal to all or any part of the period of such default or breach and the time for Producer to mail written notice to Artist pursuant to Paragraph 2 and the date of commencement of subsequent Contract Years shall be deemed extended accordingly.

13. Producer shall be responsible for payment of mechanical copyright royalties directly to the copyright proprietors. Artist shall assist Producer in obtaining mechanical licenses from the copyright proprietors of the Compositions embodied upon the Sides delivered to Producer hereunder, which licenses shall be in the general form utilized by the Harry Fox Agency, Inc., or otherwise acceptable to Producer.

14. Artist will not during the Term record, authorize, or knowingly permit to be recorded for any purpose any performance without in each case taking reasonable measures to prevent the manufacture, distribution, and sale at any time by any person other than Producer and/or the distribution company of phonograph records and other devices for home use and/or juke box use, and/or use on

or in means of transportation embodying such performance. Specifically, without limiting the generality of the foregoing, Artist agrees that:

(a) If, during the Term, Artist performs any composition for the purpose of making transcriptions for radio or television or soundtracks for motion picture films, or

(b) If, during the period referred to in Paragraph 5(b), Artist performs for any such purpose any Composition which shall have been recorded pursuant to this agreement, Artist will do so only pursuant to a written contract containing an express provision that neither such performance nor any recording thereof will be used, directly or indirectly, for the purpose of making phonograph records or any other device for home, use, and/or juke box use, and/or use on or in means of transportation. Artist will promptly furnish to Producer a copy of the pertinent provisions of each such contract and will cooperate fully with Producer in any controversy which may arise or litigation which may be brought relating to the rights of Producer under this paragraph.

15. Artist agrees that in all of Artist's endeavors in the entertainment field, Artist will exert best efforts to be billed, advertised and described as an Exclusive Recording Artist of the record company designated by Producer.

16. Artist agrees that Artist is, or will become, and that Artist will remain during the Term a member in good standing of any labor unions with which Producer may at any time have agreements lawfully requiring such union membership.

17. Artist represents and warrants that the musical compositions subject hereto will be original and will not infringe upon any other musical or literary material or upon any rights of any third party, and Artist agrees to save and hold Producer harmless from and against any and all liability, damage, cost or expense (including reasonable attorneys' fees) which Producer may pay or incur by reason of any breach or claim of breach of Artist's warranties.

18. All notices hereunder required to be given to Producer shall be sent to Producer at:

GREATER CHRIST PUBLISHING

_____

_____

and all royalties, statements and payments, and any and all notices to Artist shall be sent to Artist at:

FORMS

Artist's address, or such other address as each party respectively may hereafter designate by notice in writing to the other. All notices except royalty statements shall be sent via certified or registered mail/return receipt requested. The day of mailing of any such notice shall be deemed the date of the giving thereof.

19. No default hereunder shall be deemed material unless the party claiming such default shall give notice of such claim to the party against whom such default is claimed in writing by certified mail, return receipt requested, and unless the party against whom such default is claimed shall fail to cure the same within thirty (30) days after receipt of such notice.

IN WITNESS WHEREOF, the parties hereto have executed this agreement the day and year first above written.

PRODUCER(S)   ARTIST

BY _____   BY _____
   GREATER CHRIST PUBLISHING   PETER PAUL

SONGWRITERS AGREEMENT

AGREEMENT made this _____ day of _____ , 1994, between GREATER CHRIST PUBLISHING (hereinafter called the "Publisher") and PETER PAUL, jointly and/or severally (hereinafter called "Writer(s)"):

WITNESSETH:

In consideration of the agreement herein contained and of the sum of One ($1.00) Dollar and other good and valuable consideration in hand paid by the Publisher to the Writer(s), receipt of which is hereby acknowledged, the parties agree as follows:

1. The Writer(s) hereby sells, assigns, transfers and delivers to the Publisher, its successors and assigns, a certain heretofore unpublished original musical composition, written and/or composed by the above named Writer(s), now entitled as attached hereto:

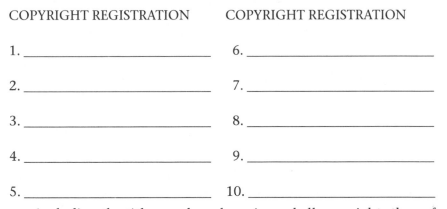

COPYRIGHT REGISTRATION   COPYRIGHT REGISTRATION

1. _____   6. _____

2. _____   7. _____

3. _____   8. _____

4. _____   9. _____

5. _____   10. _____

including the title, words and music, and all copyrights thereof, including but not limited to the copyright registration thereof No. _____ , and all rights, claims and demands in any way relating thereto, whether legal or equitable, including but not limited to the grand rights (which include, among other rights, the right to include said composition in a dramatic-musical work or review), and the exclusive right to secure copyrights therein throughout the entire world, and to have and to hold said copyrights and all rights of whatsoever nature now and hereafter thereunder existing and/or existing under any agreements or licenses relating thereto, for and during the full terms of all of said copyrights. In consideration of the agreement herein contained and the additional sum of One ($1.00) Dollar and other good and valuable consideration in hand paid by the Publisher to the Writer(s), receipt of which is hereby acknowledged, the Writer(s) hereby sells, assigns, transfers and delivers to the Publisher, its successors and assigns, the copyright of said musical composition(s) whether now known or hereafter created throughout the world to which the Writer(s) may be entitled now or hereafter, and all registrations thereof, and all rights of any and every nature now and hereafter thereunder existing for the full terms of copyrights.

2. If any of the compositions referred to herein was, in whole or part, subsisting in its original term of copyright as of January 1, 1978, Writer(s) shall so notify Publisher in writing and shall be entitled to demand as further consideration in connection therewith the additional sum of One ($1.00) Dollar, and Publisher shall be entitled to all rights of renewal and extension of copyright therein and shall be empowered as attorney in fact for Writer(s), through any officer or employee of Publisher, to renew, pursuant to law, in the name of Writer(s), if living, the copyright in said composition and to execute and deliver in the name of Writer(s), a formal assignment of each such renewal copyright to the Publisher, or to its assigns, under the terms and conditions hereof.

3. The Writer(s) hereby warrants that the said composition is his sole, exclusive, and original work, and that he has full right and power to make the within agreement, and that there exists no adverse claims to or in the said composition.

4. The Writer(s) hereby warrants that the foregoing musical composition does not infringe any other copyrighted work and has been created by the joint collaboration of the Writers named herein and that said composition, including the title, words and music thereof, has been, unless herein otherwise specifically noted, the result of the joint efforts of all the undersigned Writers and not by way of any independent or separate activity by any of the Writers.

5. In consideration of this agreement, the Publisher agrees to pay the Writer(s) One ($1.00) Dollar and other good and valuable consideration to enter into said agreement.

6. It is understood and agreed by and between all the parties hereto that all sums hereunder payable jointly to the Writer(s) shall be paid to and divided amongst them respectively as follows:

NAME	SHARE %
Peter Paul	_____

7. In the event that Publisher, within one (1) year from the date hereof, has not performed at least one of the following acts:

    (a) published and offered the musical composition for sale in regular piano copies or other customary form of trade publication; or

    (b) caused a commercial phonograph record embodying the musical composition to be made and distributed; or

    (c) licensed the use of the musical composition or any part thereof in or as part of a motion picture, or television picture, or live production, or dramatic or musical production; or

    (d) paid to the Writer(s) the sum of Fifty ($50.00) Dollars as an advance against all royalties hereunder.

    Then, subject to the provisions of Paragraph 9 herein, the Writer(s) shall have the option to give Publisher, by certified mail, written notice to the effect Publisher shall have thirty (30) days after receipt of such notice from the Writer(s) in which to cure such failure by performing any one of the acts contained in subparagraphs a), b), c) or d) of this paragraph. In the event that Publisher shall not cure such failure within the thirty (30) day period, then all rights in and to the musical composition shall automatically revert to Writer(s) without any further liability on the part of Publisher hereunder and subject to all licenses previously given by Publisher hereunder, provided that Publisher shall then advise such licensees to account directly to Writer(s) for any uses under their licenses, and if an advance is then outstanding in favor of such any licensee, Publisher shall remain liable to Writer(s) for the royalties herein stipulated if provision is not made for direct payment notwithstanding such advance.

8. The Writer(s) hereby consents to such changes, adaptations, dramatizations, transpositions, editing, and arrangements of said composition and the setting of words to the music and of music to the words, and the change of title as the Publisher deems desirable. In the event that the composition covered by this agreement is an instrumental composition, then and in such event the Writer(s) hereby irrevocably grants to the Publisher the sole and exclusive right and privilege to cause to have lyrics written for such composition by a writer or writers designated by the Publisher, which lyrics shall require only the approval of the Publisher, whereupon the Writer(s) shall be entitled to only one-half of the aforementioned royalties provided in this agreement. The Writer(s) hereby waive any and all claims which they have or may have against the

Publisher and/or its associates, affiliates, and subsidiary corporations by reason of the fact that the title may be the same or similar to that of any musical composition or compositions heretofore or hereafter acquired by the Publisher and/or its associates, affiliates, and subsidiary corporations. The Writer(s) consents to the use of his (their) name and likeness and the title to the said composition on and for the music, folios, recordings, performances, and player rolls of said composition and in connection with publicity and advertising concerning the Publisher, its successors, assigns, and licensees, and said composition and agrees that the use of such name, likeness and title may commence prior to publication and may continue so long as the Publisher shall own and/or exercise any rights in said composition.

9. Writer(s) understands and agrees that in order to exploit effectively the said composition it is frequently necessary for the Publisher, or Writer(s), pursuant to instructions from the Publisher, to make recordings of the said composition for demonstration purposes. Said recordings are, in the trade, commonly referred to as "demo records." Writer(s) agrees that effective from the date hereof, Publisher shall charge to Writer(s) and deduct from any royalty otherwise payable to Writer(s) (or in equal portions from each Writer, if there be more than one) one-half (1/2) of the costs of production of demo-records embodying the said composition. If a demo-record has been paid for by Publisher, the provisions in Paragraph 7 shall not apply, unless costs of the demo-record have been reimbursed or recouped.

10. Written demands and notices other than royalty statements provided for herein shall be sent by certified mail to the Publisher at:

Greater Christ Publishing
_____
Detroit, MI 48_____

and any and all notices to Artist shall be sent by certified mail to Artist at:

_____
_____
_____

11. Any legal action brought by the Publisher against any alleged infringer of said composition shall be initiated and prosecuted at the Publisher's sole expense, and of any recovery made by it as a

result thereof, after deduction of the expense of the litigation, a sum equal to fifty per cent (50%) shall be paid to the Writer(s).

(a) If a claim is presented against the Publisher in respect of said composition, and because thereof the Publisher is jeopardized, it shall thereupon serve written notice upon the Writer(s), containing the full details of such claim known to the Publisher, and thereafter until the claim has been adjudicated or settled, shall hold any moneys coming due the Writer(s) in escrow pending the outcome of such claim or claims. The Publisher shall have the right to settle or otherwise dispose of such claims in any manner as it in its sole discretion may determine. In the event of any recovery against the Publisher either by way of judgment or settlement, all of the costs, charges, disbursements, attorney fees, and the amount of the judgment or settlement may be deducted by the Publisher from any and all royalties or other payments theretofore or thereafter payable to the Writer(s) by the Publisher or by its associated, affiliated, or subsidiary corporations.

(b) From and after the service of summons in a suit for infringement filed against the Publisher with respect to said composition, any and all payments thereafter coming due the Writer(s) shall be held by the Publisher in trust until the suit has been adjudicated and then be disbursed accordingly, unless the Writer(s) shall elect to file an acceptable bond in the sum of payments, in which event the amounts due shall be paid to the Writer(s).

12. "Writer" as used herein shall be deemed to include all authors and composers signing this agreement.

13. The Writer(s), each for himself, hereby irrevocably constitutes and appoints the Publisher or any of its officers, directors, or general manager(s), his (their) attorney and representative, in the name(s) of the Writer(s), or any of them, or in the name of the Publisher, its successors and assigns, to make, sign, execute, acknowledge, and deliver any and all instruments which may be desirable or necessary in order to vest in the Publisher, its successors and assigns, any of the rights hereinabove referred to.

14. The Publisher shall have the right to assign this agreement and its obligations hereunder, or sell, assign, transfer, license or otherwise dispose of any of its rights and obligations in whole or in part under this agreement to any person, firm, or corporation, but said

disposition shall not affect the right of the Writer(s) to receive the royalties hereinabove set forth from the assignee.

15. This agreement shall be construed only under the laws of the State of Michigan. If any part of this agreement shall be invalid or unenforceable, it shall not affect the validity of the balance of this agreement.

16. This agreement shall be binding upon and shall inure to the benefit of the respective parties hereto, their respective successors in interest, legal representatives and assigns, and represents the entire understanding between the parties.

17. If the said composition has been recorded and released, please provide the following information:

Date and place of first release: _____

Record Company: _____

Record number: _____

IN WITNESS WHEREOF, the parties hereto have hereunto set their hands and seals the day and year first above written.

PUBLISHER   WRITER

BY _____   _____

GREATER CHRIST PUBLISHING   PETER PAUL

SPONSOR PROPOSAL

"AN EVENING WITH JOHN AMOS & NOEL POINTER"
AN EXTRAORDINARY EVENT
1986/1987 TOUR SERIES

From: **Gregory J. Reed, ESQ.**
Gregory J. Reed & Associates, P.C.
1201 Bagley
Detroit, Michigan 48226
(313) 961-3580

Table of Information

Introduction

During 1986/1987 Gregory J. Reed of Gregory J. Reed and Associates will produce and tour "An Evening with John Amos & Noel Pointer," an extraordinary evening with music/theatrics, an evening to remember. The following outlines the potential benefits created through participation as the event's primary sponsor.

Demographics

The demographics of the individuals who attend an event designed with theater and music, a quasi-concert are: diverse in ages; very upscale in education, earning broad ranges of income; and fall within the professional/managerial, as well as blue collar categories. The event creates a very unique mix.

It is estimated that approximately 40,000 persons in Michigan alone will see "An Evening with John Amos & Noel Pointer." This event will tour major cities in Michigan, and an additional 20,000,000 plus impressions will be developed from the event and aggressive advertising/promotional campaign in Michigan and other states.

The event will be on tour throughout the midwest in the following states: Michigan, Ohio, Illinois, Wisconsin and Minnesota prior to touring the eastern states and the western border states.

Preview of Sponsor's Benefits Associated with the Tour Event

A) Reasonable marketing cost;
B) Product presence being exhibited in various regions on tour, not an isolated presence tied to one site—ubiquitous effect;
C) Maintain and increase market penetration or position of gains;
D) Product identification with a positive cultured and artistic community event;
E) Increase awareness for your product(s);
F) Aligning the company's image with two internationally renowned Americans, the company is able to reach consumers that attend the event and draw attention to others who are followers of John Amos and Noel Pointer—both are known by persons of various professions, incomes, ages and all races.
G) Demographic ages range from 15 to 65; and
H) Visibility of the company's image throughout the media industry.

Benefits

As a Primary Sponsor for the tour series or a specific event site, the SPONSOR will receive:

A) Credit line, SPONSOR'S name in association with product "..." in 100% of the program's newspaper and magazine advertising.
B) Credit line, SPONSOR's name in association with "..." in 100% of radio program advertising.
C) Theater or facility presence, i.e., display space and/or exhibition of graphics within the facility.
D) Full page black and white advertisement within the program publication.

E) A bonus in publicity rights, i.e., the right to advertise or promote this association and relationship by way of TV, T-shirts, etc.

F) Credit line, SPONSOR's name in association with "..." in the prepared posters and flyers.

G) Product/Service exclusivity, i.e., you as sponsor will be the only company involved within your product/service category.

H) Names/Logos shall be inserted on items or paraphernalia connected with promotion of the "Event" and press releases.

I) Promotion as artists exhibit or use your product as a part of the performance.

J) Discount of 20% to sponsor's employees for ticket purchases—morale booster.

K) A minimum of four tickets to event per show.

Basic Contract Terms and Conditions

- Total Michigan sponsorship fee payable in cash.
- Fee per other sites or states shall be negotiated and structured once agreed upon.
- Payment is due within ten (10) days upon contract execution.

EMPLOYMENT OF MINISTER CONTRACT

THIS EMPLOYMENT AGREEMENT ("Agreement"), is made as of the 1st day of _____1994, between _____ CHURCH, a non-profit corporation (the "Church"), and BISHOP _____ State of _____ , hereinafter referred to as ("Bishop _____").

WITNESSETH

WHEREAS, the Church has employed and wishes to continue to employ Bishop _____ upon the terms and conditions contained in this Agreement; and

WHEREAS, Bishop _____ is willing to accept such employment upon the terms and conditions contained in this Agreement;

NOW THEREFORE, in consideration of the premises and the mutual agreements hereinafter set forth, the parties hereto hereby agree as follows:

1. **Duties and Extent of Services.** The Church agrees to employ Bishop _____ , and Bishop _____ agrees to accept employment, for an initial term of (20) years from the date of this Agreement. During the term of this Agreement, Bishop _____ agrees to serve as Pastor of the Church and to abide by the Constitution and Bylaws of the Church.

2. **Activities During Employment.** Bishop _____ shall devote such portion of his time, energy, and skill as are necessary and appropriate to the performance of his duties under the Constitution and Bylaws of the Church (with vacations as provided and reasonable absences because of illness excepted). During the term of this Agreement and unless otherwise expressly authorized herein, Bishop _____ will not, without the express consent of the Church, in accordance with its Constitution and Bylaws, engage in or be otherwise directly or indirectly interested in any activity detrimental to the best interests of the Church or any civic, political or other outside activities which prevent Bishop _____ from devoting sufficient time, energy, and skill to the performance of his duties of the Church.

3. **Compensation.** For serving as Pastor of the Church, Bishop shall be paid and furnished with the following renumeration and benefits:

   (a) Love Offering. The Church agrees to continue its practice of having one offering per week at Sunday service to be considered a gratuitous "love offering" from the membership to the

Pastor, _____ , to be kept by him as a gift from the membership at such service.

(b) **Salary.** Beginning on the fifth (5th) day of the month following the month in which the Church's loan from _____ is a participant (evidenced by a note, the "Mutual Note," dated _____) is paid in full, the Church shall pay Bishop _____ , as salary, the sum of _____ dollars per month, and continuing for the duration of Bishop _____ employment (including vacation periods and any periods of illness or temporary disability), said monthly salary to be reviewed by Bishop _____ and the Board of Trustees each year beginning one year after said salary payment begin, to be adjusted upward if deemed appropriate after such review. In addition, beginning immediately after the Mutual Note is paid in full, Bishop _____ shall receive, personally, all revenues and compensation resulting from revival meetings conducted by him, and the Church shall have no right in or claim to said revenues and compensation, said revenues and compensation thereafter to be Bishop _____ revenues and compensation for his services in conducting such revivals. In the event of Bishop _____ permanent disability, as defined and determined under subparagraph (c) below, Bishop _____ shall, regardless of whether the Mutual Note has been paid in full, be paid a salary of no less than _____ dollars per month beginning one month from the first date of his actual permanent disability and continuing until his death or the termination of such permanent disability, said salary to be in addition to all other disability benefits to which Bishop _____ is entitled under this Agreement or outside this Agreement.

(c) **Deferred Compensation.** It is recognized that Bishop ____ _____ has made significant contributions to the Church, not only in terms of his time, effort, and services, but also in terms of the significant revenues which he has generated for the Church and for which he received no personal compensation. In recognition of such services and the personal and financial sacrifices and contributions made by Bishop _____ , the Church hereby agrees to pay to Bishop _____ (or to his heirs, executors, administrators or assigns) upon the termination of his employment with the Church for any reason other than permanent disability (including, but not limited to, the death, incompetency, retirement, or discharge from employment, with or without cause), a sum equal to the difference between the sum of _____ and the total amount of any salary payment previously made to Bishop _____ under paragraph 3(b) above (said difference being hereinafter referred to as the "Deferred Compensation Amount"). The Deferred Compensation Amount shall be in five (5) equal annual installments. The first payment of such deferred compensation shall be paid ninety (90) days after the date of termination of Bishop _____ employment. Each of the four remaining installments shall be paid on each of the four next succeeding anniversary dates of the termination of Bishop _____ employment. Anything heretofore to the contrary notwithstanding, if Bishop _____ employment is terminated as a result of permanent disability on his part, the Church shall pay the Deferred Compensation Amount to him (or to his guardian or committee appointed by law), in equal installments of _____ dollars per year until the Deferred Compensation Amount is paid in full; provided, however, that if the quotient that results from dividing the Deferred Compensation Amount by five (5) results in an amount less than _____ said quotient amount shall be paid to Bishop _____ each year for the five year period following his permanent disability. In the event that Bishop _____ dies during such period of permanent disability, the unpaid balance of the Deferred Compensation Amount shall be paid to Bishop _____ heirs, executives, and assigns in annual installments at the rate of dollars (per annum), with the first installment payment due ninety (90) days after the date of Bishop _____ death, until the total Deferred Compensation Amount due Bishop under this Paragraph 3(b) has been paid in full. For purposes of determining whether Bishop _____ is permanently disabled, he shall be deemed to be disabled for the purposes of this Agreement if he is determined to be disabled under the terms and provisions of disability insurance policy number issued to Bishop _____ by Insurance Company. If such disability insurance policy is no longer in effect, or if a determination of Bishop _____ disability cannot be made under such policy for any reason, the Church may, if it wishes to do so, rely upon a certification of permanent disability made by Bishop _____ personal physician or such other physician as Bishop _____ may select. If the Church does not wish to rely upon a physician chosen by Bishop _____ , Bishop _____ shall be deemed to be disabled for purposes of this Agreement if he shall be certified as being disabled by two of three physicians chosen as follows. Church shall (within ten (10) days after receiving written notice from Bishop _____ or his duly appointed guardian, committee, or other "personal representative") appoint a physician licensed to practice medicine in the State of _____ ; within such period of time Bishop _____ or his personal representative shall select such a physician; within ten (10) days after the date of the selection of the Church's physician, the Church's physician and Bishop _____ physician shall by agreement, select a third physician licensed to practice medicine in the State of _____ . Within twenty (20) days after the third physician is selected, the three physicians so selected shall make or cause to be made such examination of Bishop _____ as they deem appropriate and shall each state his or her opinion and decision as to whether or not Bishop _____ is so disabled as to be incapable of performing his duties as Pastor of the Church. The opinion and decision of two or more of such physicians shall govern the determination of disability for purposes of this Agreement.

(d) **Parsonage.** The Church hereby agrees to furnish to Bishop _____ , free of any cost or expense on his part, a home and residence to be occupied by him and his family (hereinafter referred to as the "parsonage"). The Church is presently furnishing Bishop _____ with the parsonage located on _____ , _____ , _____ County, _____ . The Church agrees to continue to make all payments and to otherwise continue to furnish such Parsonage to Bishop _____ free of any cost or expenses on Bishop _____ part; and, in the event Bishop _____ desires to change his residence from time to time, the Church agrees to furnish him with a parsonage at least comparable to the present parsonage on _____ . The Church further agrees that Bishop _____ and his children (during their father's life, or after his death, or in the event Bishop _____ shall die, during the minority of his children) shall have the right, free of any cost or expense on his (or their) part, to occupy any such parsonage for so long as he (or they) wish to do so and notwithstanding the termination of Bishop _____ employment for any reason (including, but not limited to, his death, disability, incompetency, retirement or discharge, whether or not for cause). The Church agrees that to protect and reflect his rights in and to any such parsonage, Bishop _____ may, at his election, record this Agreement on the real property records of County, _____ . The Church agrees to make such other and further conveyances to Bishop _____ as Bishop _____ might deem necessary or appropriate to carry out the terms of this Agreement respecting the parsonage.

(e) **Automobile.** The Church shall furnish Bishop _____ with a new automobile at such intervals as Bishop _____ and the Board of Trustees of the Church shall agree, but in no event less than every three (3) years. The Church shall also pay for all operating costs of such vehicle including, but not limited to, gasoline, oil, tires, repairs, and other costs of operation. In the event Bishop _____ employment is terminated for any reason (including, but not limited to, death, disability, incompetency, retirement or discharge, whether or not for cause), Bishop _____ (or if he is deceased, disabled or incompetent, his wife) shall be entitled to keep, free of charge, the automobile that he is then operating pursuant to this Agreement; and Bishop _____ (or his wife) shall thenceforth be responsible for the costs of operating such vehicle.

(f) **Tax Shelter Annuity.** The Church shall make annual contributions to the tax shelter annuity covering Bishop _____ with Insurance Company. Such annual contributions shall be equal to the maximum amount of such a contribution that can be excluded by Bishop _____ from his gross income for federal income tax purposes. Bishop _____ shall have all rights and powers over and in such annuity contract (including the designation of beneficiaries) that can be given to him from time to time without jeopardizing the favorable tax treatment granted to tax shelter annuities.

(g) **Vacation.** Bishop _____ shall have one month of vacation, with full pay and benefits, during the month of December, each year, and during other periods within his discretion up to a maximum of three (3) months per year.

(h) **Life and Disability Insurance.** During the term of this Agreement, the Church shall pay all premiums and keep in force the whole life insurance policies on Bishop _____ and his family shown on Schedule "A" which is attached hereto and incorporated by reference herein. Said policies and Schedule "A" may be changed from time to time by mutual agreement of the parties hereto. The Church's obligation to pay the premiums on each policy shown on Schedule "A" shall terminate only upon the death of the insured, or in the case of any policy upon Bishop _____ spouse, upon the issuance of a valid decree of divorce to either of such parties. Bishop _____ shall have the sole and exclusive right to designate the beneficiary under each such policy shown on Schedule "A."

(i) During the term of this Agreement, the Church shall pay all premiums and keep in force the individual disability insurance policy issued by Insurance Company (Policy No. _____) covering Bishop _____ . Any benefits or proceeds of such policy shall be paid as Bishop _____ may from time to time direct. The Church's obligation to pay the premiums upon such policy shall terminate only upon Bishop _____ death.

4. **Expenses.** Bishop _____ shall be reimbursed by the Church for all expenses reasonably incurred by him in connection with the performance of his duties as Pastor, including, but not limited to, expenses for travel, business meals, entertainment, and similar items, upon presentation from time to time of itemized statements of such expenses.

5. **Church Debts.** The Church acknowledges that the indebtedness due _____ , respectively, copies of which are attached hereto, are debts of the Church and will be repaid by the Church as and when due (if not sooner), even though Bishop _____ signature appears on such notes as the borrower.

6. **Key Person Insurance.** The parties recognize Bishop _____ importance to the Church and acknowledge that the Church has an insurable interest in Bishop _____ should it wish to purchase key person insurance upon his life.

7. **Term.** The term of this Agreement shall begin on the date first above written and shall run for a period of ____ years from the date hereof, unless earlier terminated by Agreement of the parties or unless Bishop _____ gives written notice to the Church ninety (90) days in advance that he wishes to voluntarily terminate his employment with the Church. Such voluntary termination of employment by Bishop _____ shall not nullify the Church's obligations under paragraph 2 of this Agreement, including, but not limited to, obligations regarding deferred compensation, the parsonage, the automobile, and insurance.

8. **Waiver of Breach.** The waiver by either party of a breach of any provision of this Agreement shall not operate or be construed as a

waiver of any subsequent breach of the same or any other provision by the offending party.

9. **Severability.** If any provision of this Agreement shall be held invalid or unenforceable by any court of competent jurisdiction, such holding shall not invalidate or render unenforceable any other provision hereof.

10. **Benefit.** This Agreement shall be binding upon and inure to the benefit of, and be enforceable by the heirs, legal representatives, successors, transferees and assigns of the parties hereto.

11. **Notice and Communications.** Any notice required or permitted to be given pursuant to this Agreement shall be deemed properly given if in writing and personally delivered or deposited, postage prepaid, in a regularly maintained receptacle for United States Mail, certified mail, return receipt requested, and directed to:____

_____

_____ .

Addresses for notice purposes may be changed by a written notice in the manner described above for notices.

12. **Entire Agreement.** This Agreement constitutes the entire agreement among the parties hereto with respect to the subject matter hereof. No modification or amendment to this agreement shall be deemed effective unless in writing and signed by both parties.

13. **Applicable Law.** This Agreement shall be construed and the legal relations between the parties determined in accordance with the laws of the State of Michigan.

14. **Counterparts.** This Agreement may be executed in one or more counterparts, each of which shall be deemed to be an original, but all of which together shall constitute one and the same instrument.

IN WITNESS WHEREOF, the Church has caused this Agreement to be duly approved, executed and delivered in its behalf in accordance with its Constitution and Bylaws and has caused its proper corporate seal to be affixed hereto, and Bishop _____ has duly executed, sealed and delivered this Agreement, all as of the day and year first above written.

Subscribed before me this _____
day of _____ , 1994

_____   _____ CHURCH

Notary Public

_____   By:_____

Unofficial Witness   Trustee and Designated Officer

(Corporate Seal)

Subscribed before me this _____
day of _____ , 1994

_____   _____
Notary Public   Attest: Church Clerk

Subscribed before me this _____
day of _____ , 1994

_____   _____
Notary Public   Bishop

                                             (SEAL)

_____
Unofficial Witness

FORMS

Schedule "A"

INSURANCE POLICIES
ON THE LIFE OF
BISHOP _____ AND HIS FAMILY

    1. Insurance Company
       Policy No.: _____

    2. Insurance Company
       Policy No.: _____

INDEPENDENT CHOIR DIRECTOR AGREEMENT

AGREEMENT made this _____ day of _____ , 199___ between COMMUNITY A.M.E. CHURCH of 4010 17th Street, Ecorse, Michigan and _____ , the undersigned.

WHEREAS, the undersigned is desirous of performing services as a Choir Director and the undersigned is desirous to enter into this agreement with respect to the terms hereto follow with COMMUNITY A.M.E. CHURCH.

NOW, THEREFORE, in consideration of the premises and of the mutual agreement hereinafter set forth, the parties hereby agree as follows:

1. **TERM:** This agreement shall cover a week-to-week period subject to being extended by the parties.
2. **DUTIES:** The undersigned shall render services to the Church as a Choir Director and shall assist with the Church's services.
3. **COMPENSATION:** The Church shall pay the Choir Director for services rendered a fee of $ _____ per each Sunday service or an amount agreed upon between the parties per the occasion in which the Choir Director has agreed to perform services.
4. **RELATIONSHIP BETWEEN PARTIES:** The Choir Director is retained and is to perform services only in the manner as set forth herein and the relationship during the period of this agreement shall be that of an independent party, said party is free to dispose of such portion of one's entire time, energy, and skills during regular business hours as the party is obligated to devote hereunder as a Choir Director in such a manner as the person sees fit. The Church agrees that this contract does not call for all or the exclusive time or services of said Choir Director. The Choir Director shall not be considered under provisions of this agreement or otherwise as having employee status. The Church shall not withhold taxes, Choir Director shall be responsible for payment of taxes and obligations as an independent party as specified for independent parties performing services as under the Internal Revenue Code, state and municipal laws. The Choir Director shall receive a 1099 NEC statement if payment exceeds $600.00 during the calendar year.
5. **SCHEDULING/SUPPLIES:** The Choir Director shall provide his/her own instrument(s) and supplies. The Church shall have no control over scheduling the practice and rehearsal sessions of the Choir Director. The Choir Director can perform services for other

parties which do not interfere with the Church's activities or assignments.

6. **TERMINATION:** This agreement may be terminated at any time by either party upon five (5) days' notice to the other party. In the event that the undersigned violates any of the provisions of this agreement or fails to perform the services required of him/her by this agreement, then at the option of the Church this agreement shall at once cease and terminate. The Church shall be under no obligation to the said undersigned Choir Director except to pay him/her such compensation as he/she may be entitled to receive up to the time of such termination.

7. **ARBITRATION:** Any controversy or claim arising out of, or relating to, this agreement or the breach thereof, shall be settled by arbitration in accordance with the rules then obtaining of the American Arbitration Association, and judgment upon the award rendered may be entered in any court having jurisdiction thereof.

IN WITNESS WHEREOF, we have hereunto set our hands this _____ day of _____ , 199___.

_____   _____
Independent Choir Director   Community A.M.E. Church

RESOLUTIONS

Parsonage Resolution

WHEREAS, the Reverend John H. Payne, an ordained minister serves the MT. VERNON M.B. CHURCH, located at 3740 Jos Campau in Detroit, Michigan in the performance of sacredotal functions and in the conduct of religious worship, and

WHEREAS, the MT. VERNON M.B. CHURCH does not provide a residence for its appointed minister.

IT IS HEREBY RESOLVED that the total compensation to be paid to Rev. John H. Payne for the period of January, 19__ and ending December, 19__ and other periods shall be resolved by the Church upon any increase to be paid to Rev. John H. Payne. The Church will provide parsonage allowance for Rev. John H. Payne covering his total compensation, said payment shall be for his parsonage allowance since the Church does not provide a residence for him. Said payment shall be for $920.00 to cover his expenses for his shelter during the said period. The payment will cover the following items as follows:

a) real estate taxes,
b) utilities,
c) insurance,
d) garbage removal,
e) maintenance,
f) home furnishings, and
g) any additional expenses that are directly related to operating his shelter as a parsonage.

FURTHER RESOLVED, that the Church will reimburse Rev. John H. Payne for his travel expenses incurred and incidentals related thereto in the amount of $1,500 for the year of 19__; said amount will be increased based upon inflation.

There being no further business, this resolution being approved and accepted, the meeting was adjourned.

Dated: January 2, 19__   _____

FORMS

Expense Account

Please be advised that the Board of Trustees and the Board of Deacons have called a Special Meeting to be held at their office of the church at 3184 W. Pierson Road, Flint, Michigan 48504 on the ____ day of _____ , 19 ___ , at _____ __ .m., for the purpose of considering to defray certain incidental and administrative expenses incurred by REV. FRED WHITE.

WHEREAS, the church deems that it would be appropriate in order for the minister to carry out his ecclesiastical duties in fulfillment of his obligation to the congregation.

WHEREAS, the Trustees are considering authorization of payment to defray such incurring costs.

WHEREAS, the Board has received the necessary operating expenses and is considering opening a checking account to meet such obligations as incurred by REV. FRED WHITE.

RESOLVED, the church's Board deems it to be appropriate and necessary to designate and authorize such persons and empowers them to open an expense account with a financial institution to be designated by such persons as an expense account for REV. FRED WHITE.

(Re: Expense Account)

RESOLVED, the Board of Trustees and Board of Deacons have approved an Expense Account for REV. FRED WHITE. He shall receive monies that are necessary and appropriate that he incurs in facilitating matters on behalf of the church which may be direct or incidental. Any person(s) that takes note of this Resolution can rely upon it to be effective and in full force as of the date of execution.

There being no further business, the meeting was adjourned.

IN WITNESS WHEREOF, we have set our hands this _____ day of _____ , 19___ .

_____   _____

_____   _____

_____   _____

Endnotes

Chapter 2
1. Clergy, Tax and Law, Inc., p. 28.
2. Howard L. Oleck, *Nonprofit Corporations, Organizations, and Associations,* 3d ed. (New York: Prentice-Hall, 1975), p. 73.
3. Ibid., p. 495.
4. Ibid., p. 365.
5. Ibid., p. R7–128.
6. Ibid., p. 63.
7. Ibid., pp. 584–85.

Chapter 3
8. Reg. Sec. 7611.
9. Reg. Sec. 170(c) of the Internal Revenue Code of 1954.
10. Reg. Sec. 7611(e).
11. Temporary Reg. 301.7611–1T, A–5.
12. Reg. Sec. 7611(b)(4).
13. Reg. Sec. 1.513–1(d)(2).
14. Reg. Sec. 512(b)(12).
15. Reg. Sec. 162.
16. Reg. Sec. 1.513–1(c)(1).
17. *Suffolk County Patrolmen's Benevolent Assn.* 77 TC 1314.
18. Reg. Sec. 1.513–1(c)(i).
19. Reg. Sec. 1.513–1(c)(i).
20. *Rensselaer Polytechnic Institute v. Comm.* (2 Circuit, 1984), 53 AFTRD 84–1167.
21. ??
22. *Universal Church of Jesus Christ, Inc., and Dona Sly, Director v. Comm.* (Feb. 23, 1991, T.C. Memo, 1988–65).
23. Reg. Sec. 7805(b).
24. Reg. Sec. 1.512(b)–1(i).
25. Reg. Sec. 512(b)(4).
26. Reg. Sec. 1.514(b)–1(a).
27. Reg. Sec. 1.514(b)–1(b)(i).
28. Reg. Sec. 1.514(b)–1(b)(ii).
29. *Gunderson Medical Foundation, Ltd. v. U.S.* (DC Wis., 1982), 49 AFTR2d 82–1125.
30. Letter Ruling 81450011.
31. Reg. Sec. 1.514(b)–1(b)(4).
32. Reg. Sec. 1.514(b)–1(b)(5).
33. Reg. Sec. 1.514(b)–1(2)(c).
34. Reg. Sec. 1.514(b)–1(d)(iii).
35. Reg. Sec. 512(c).
36. Reg. Sec. 1.512(b)–1(c).

37. Reg. Sec. 512(b)(5).
38. *Tax Exempt Organizations* (New York: Prentice-Hall), 16,246.
39. Reg. Sec. 501(c)(5) and (6)).
40. Reg. Sec. 1.512(a)–1(d).
41. *Florida Trucking Association, Inc.,* 87 TC 1039.
42. *Fraternal Order of Police, Illinois State Troopers Lodge No. 41* v. *Comm.* (7th Circuit 1987), 60 AFTR2d 87–6050.
43. *U.S.* v. *American College of Physicians* (1986), 57 AFRTD 86 1182.
44. Reg. Sec. 1.512(a)–1(f).
45. Reg. Sec. 513(f).
46. Reg. Sec. 1.513–5(b).
47. *Waco Lodge No. 166, B.P.O.E.* v. *Comm.* (5th Circuit, 1983), 51 AFTRD 629.
48. Letter Ruling 8206031.
49. Letter Ruling 8038020.
50. Letter Ruling 8215033.
51. Reg. Sec. 513(h).
52. Reg. Sec. 513(d)(2)(c).
53. Reg. Sec. 1.513(c)(2).
54. Reg. Sec. 1.513–3(c)(3).
55. Reg. Sec. 513(a)(1).
56. Reg. Sec. 513(c)(3).
57. Reg. Sec. 1402(c)(4).
58. Reg. Sec. 1.107(c)–.
59. *Swaggart* v. *Comm.*, 48 T.C.M. 759 (1984).
60. Reg. Sec. 501(c)(3), 170.
61. Reg. Sec. 1.162–8(b)(3).
62. *Church of Scientology* v. *Comm.*, 1987–2 USTC.
63. *Easter House* v. *U.S.*, 60 AFTR2d 87–5119 (1987).
64. *Presbyterian and Reformed Publishing Co.* v. *Comm.*, 54 AFTR2d 84–5730.
65. Reg. Sec. 3101; 6102; 3111.
66. Reg. Sec. 3102(b), 3111.
67. Reg. Sec. 6672.
68. Letter Ruling 8321053.
69. Reg. Sec. 31.3121(d)–1(c)(2).
70. Reg. Sec. 3121(a)(16).
71. Reg. Sec. 3121(b)(19).
72. Reg. Sec. 1402(d); 3101(c); 3111(c); 3121(w).
73. Reg. Sec. 3121(b)(10) and (13).
74. Reg. Sec. 1401(a) and (b).
75. Reg. Sec. 1402(b)(2).
76. Rev. Rule 70–197, 1970–1 CB 181.
77. Temporary Reg. Sec. 1.1402(e)–5T(b).
78. Title VII.
79. *Bob Jones University* v. *United States*, 461 U.S. 574 (1983).

Chapter 4
80. Peter A. H. Meggs et al., *Television–Radio–Film for Churchmen* (1969), p. 154.
81. Ibid., p. 160.

ENDNOTES

82. Charles Somervill and Kerry I. Townson, *Media Handbook for Churches* (Lousiville: Westminster /John Knox, 1988), p. 30.
83. Meggs et al., *Television–Radio–Film for Churchmen*, vol. 2, p. 73.
84. Somervill and Townson, *Media Handbook for Churches*, p. 29.
85. Meggs et al., *Television–Radio–Film for Churchmen*, p. 174.
86. Peter G. Horsfield, *Religious Television: The American Experience* (White Plains. N.Y.: Longman, 1984), p. 148.
87. Ibid., p. 157.
88. Meggs, et al., *Television-Radio-Film for Churchmen*, p. 166.

Chapter 8
89. William M. Easum, *The Church Growth Handbook* (Nashville: Abingdon, 1990), pp. 121–24.
90. Ibid., pp. 124–26.
91. Ibid., p. 128.
92. Ibid., p. 129.
93. Ibid., pp. 133–34.
94. Ibid., pp. 134–35.
95. Ibid., pp. 140–41.
96. Ibid., pp. 141–42.
97. Ibid., pp. 142–44.
98. Ibid., pp. 144–46.
99. Ibid., pp. 146–52.
100. Ibid., pp. 152–53.
101. Ibid., pp. 154–56.

About the Author

Gregory J. Reed of Gregory J. Reed & Associates, P.C. (Detroit, Michigan), has been a driving force in Michigan churches and related religious institutions for nearly two decades. From the smallest churches, to some of the largest congregations in Michigan, Reed is one of the few attorneys who has demonstrated the skill and vision to expand the functions of the church to include meeting the challenges of the church in leading society into the twenty-first century. Over the course of the years, Reed has designed and implemented organizational structure for various churches and assisted with the development of their many ancillary functions. Additionally, the author has been instrumental in obtaining tax-exempt status for religious organizations and their counterparts, as well as formalizing the church as a legal entity as defined, in part, by the contents of the materials outlined in this publication.

Reed is a practicing attorney actively specializing in corporate, tax, sports, and entertainment laws. He is used as an expert witness in contract, trademark, business, and entertainment cases throughout the United States.

Mr. Reed is also a producer and represents individuals, firms, numerous entertainers, sports figures, athletes, and artists from television to Broadway. He has negotiated contracts for athletes, entertainers, and parties connected with various media related endeavors for over 18 years.

Reed's experiences are quite diverse—he is the only attorney to represent six world boxing champions: Thomas Hearns, Hilmer Kenty, Leon Spinks, Pipino Cuevas, Tony Tucker, etc. He was instrumental in negotiating one of the largest contracts in boxing history—the $30 million Hearns v. Sugar Ray Leonard contest. Reed also negotiated the unification of the heavyweight boxing titles involving Mike Tyson and Tony Tucker.

Mr. Reed recently purchased the original manuscript of the Autobiography of Malcolm X which includes the handwritten notations of both Alex Haley and Malcolm X. He is currently in the process of establishing an exhibition and several media-related projects based on this work.

Reed was the chief lead counsel involving the first, historical multimillion dollar lawsuit against Miss USA Pageant, Inc. regarding Miss

ABOUT THE AUTHOR

Carole Gist (first black Miss USA 1990) [v. Miss Universe Pageant, Inc.] which was settled in January of 1992.

He has served as a consultant to promoters, artists, attorneys, and persons involved in sports and entertainment. He has lectured in foreign countries, as well as nationwide, on sports, entertainment laws, and motivation.

Reed has produced plays, such as the Pulitzer Prize winning production "A Soldier's Play," which was developed into a screenplay by Columbia Pictures, "A Soldier's Story." Reed has staged the largest touring entertainment tribute in the United States in honor of Dr. Martin Luther King, Jr., with Emmy Award winner Al Eaton in "We Are the Dream." Reed also produced a documentary of the Last Poets, the originators of Rap music, and was Associate Producer for the documentary concert of "The Temptations" honoring David Ruffin.

Author of six books, Mr. Reed has written the first exclusive contract negotiation guide with aspects of taxation for entertainment and sports law in the U.S. entitled *"Tax Planning and Contract Negotiating Techniques for Creative Persons, Professional Athletes and Entertainers."* The book was used by several colleges, staff members of the National Football League, the National Basketball Association, and the Major League Baseball Association. It was the only tax-planning and contract reference book cited at the American Bar Association's First Entertainment and Sports Forum as "a practical guide to taxation and related business problems of celebrities."

The author's second book, *"This Business of Boxing and Its Secrets,"* the only book of its kind, made the New York's best seller list and was cited as an international authority on the subject. *"This Business of Entertainment and Its Secrets"* is in its third printing and is used by colleges throughout the U.S. (e.g., NYU, Howard University, Florida University and Memphis University). *"Negotiations Behind Closed Doors"* (in revision for re-release) deals with the hard-hitting realities of deal making and negotiating. His most recent and fifth book *"This Business of Celebrity Estates"* (in publication) deals with preserving, marketing, and licensing memorabilia of celebrities and much more.

Reed is the first African-American lawyer to chair a Sports and Entertainment Lawyer's Section in the United States, the Michigan Bar Association. He was the first African-American lawyer to be a member of the Internal Revenue Service Advisory Board of the United States and first in Michigan to receive a Masters Degree in Taxation Law. He was selected as the legal counsel for Nelson Mandela's tour committee in Michigan. Reed is one of the founders and the former Vice-President for the Board of Black Entertainment and Sports Lawyers Association, and has been inducted in the Association's Hall of Fame.

He is also the founder of the Gregory J. Reed Scholarship Foundation that aids students in the fields of art, engineering, and law. Mr. Reed has been a professor of taxation in the School of Business at Wayne State University, Detroit, Michigan. He is the first African-American Board Member of the Michigan State University Foundation (a $50 million entity) and serves as its Treasurer and Chairperson of the Financial/Investment Committee.

Cited By:

The Detroit News as one of the top lawyers in the legal profession
Who's Who in Entertainment
Who's Who among Black Americans
Who's Who among American Lawyers
Who's Who in Finance

College Education:

B.S.   Michigan State University (Engineering)
M.S.   Michigan State University (Management Science)
J.D.   Wayne State University
L.L.M.   Wayne State University (Master of Taxation Law)